OVERSIGHT OF THE DHS HEADQUARTERS PROJECT AT ST. ELIZABETHS: IMPACT ON THE TAXPAYER

HEARING

BEFORE THE

SUBCOMMITTEE ON OVERSIGHT AND MANAGEMENT EFFICIENCY

OF THE

COMMITTEE ON HOMELAND SECURITY HOUSE OF REPRESENTATIVES

ONE HUNDRED THIRTEENTH CONGRESS

SECOND SESSION

SEPTEMBER 19, 2014

Serial No. 113–87

Printed for the use of the Committee on Homeland Security

Available via the World Wide Web: http://www.gpo.gov/fdsys/

U.S. GOVERNMENT PUBLISHING OFFICE

93–365 PDF WASHINGTON : 2015

For sale by the Superintendent of Documents, U.S. Government Publishing Office
Internet: bookstore.gpo.gov   Phone: toll free (866) 512–1800; DC area (202) 512–1800
Fax: (202) 512–2104   Mail: Stop IDCC, Washington, DC 20402–0001

COMMITTEE ON HOMELAND SECURITY

MICHAEL T. MCCAUL, Texas, *Chairman*

LAMAR SMITH, Texas
PETER T. KING, New York
MIKE ROGERS, Alabama
PAUL C. BROUN, Georgia
CANDICE S. MILLER, Michigan, *Vice Chair*
PATRICK MEEHAN, Pennsylvania
JEFF DUNCAN, South Carolina
TOM MARINO, Pennsylvania
JASON CHAFFETZ, Utah
STEVEN M. PALAZZO, Mississippi
LOU BARLETTA, Pennsylvania
RICHARD HUDSON, North Carolina
STEVE DAINES, Montana
SUSAN W. BROOKS, Indiana
SCOTT PERRY, Pennsylvania
MARK SANFORD, South Carolina
CURTIS CLAWSON, Florida

BENNIE G. THOMPSON, Mississippi
LORETTA SANCHEZ, California
SHEILA JACKSON LEE, Texas
YVETTE D. CLARKE, New York
BRIAN HIGGINS, New York
CEDRIC L. RICHMOND, Louisiana
WILLIAM R. KEATING, Massachusetts
RON BARBER, Arizona
DONALD M. PAYNE, JR., New Jersey
BETO O'ROURKE, Texas
FILEMON VELA, Texas
ERIC SWALWELL, California
VACANCY
VACANCY

BRENDAN P. SHIELDS, *Staff Director*
JOAN O'HARA, *Acting Chief Counsel*
MICHAEL S. TWINCHEK, *Chief Clerk*
I. LANIER AVANT, *Minority Staff Director*

———

SUBCOMMITTEE ON OVERSIGHT AND MANAGEMENT EFFICIENCY

JEFF DUNCAN, South Carolina, *Chairman*

PAUL C. BROUN, Georgia
LOU BARLETTA, Pennsylvania
RICHARD HUDSON, North Carolina
STEVE DAINES, Montana, *Vice Chair*
MICHAEL T. MCCAUL, Texas *(Ex Officio)*

RON BARBER, Arizona
DONALD M. PAYNE, JR., New Jersey
BETO O'ROURKE, Texas
BENNIE G. THOMPSON, Mississippi *(Ex Officio)*

RYAN CONSAUL, *Subcommittee Staff Director*
DEBORAH JORDAN, *Subcommittee Clerk*
TAMLA SCOTT, *Minority Subcommittee Staff Director*

CONTENTS

Page

OVERSIGHT OF THE DHS HEADQUARTERS PROJECT AT ST. ELIZABETHS: IMPACT ON THE TAXPAYER

Friday, September 19, 2014

U.S. House of Representatives,
Subcommittee on Oversight and
Management Efficiency,
Committee on Homeland Security,
Washington, DC.

The subcommittee met, pursuant to call, at 9:35 a.m., in Room 311, Cannon House Office Building, Hon. Jeff Duncan [Chairman of the subcommittee] presiding.

Present: Representatives Duncan, Barber, and Payne.

Also present: Representative Norton.

Mr. DUNCAN. The Committee on Homeland Security, Subcommittee on Oversight and Management Efficiency will come to order. The purpose of this hearing is to receive testimony regarding the Department of Homeland Security's consolidation project at St. Elizabeths. I will now recognize myself for an opening statement.

Since 2006 the Department of Homeland Security, DHS, and General Services Administration, GSA, have spent over a billion taxpayer dollars to build a consolidated DHS Headquarters on the St. Elizabeths campus in Southeast Washington, DC. St. Elizabeths is a National historic landmark that was originally founded in 1852 as the Government Hospital for the Insane.

The purpose of the new headquarters was to consolidate DHS leadership and operations to improve efficiency. Unfortunately, as shown by a Government Accountability Office, GAO, report that was released today, the project has become a monument to mismanagement.

DHS and GSA spent 3 years planning for the project before 1 ounce of concrete was poured. Finally, in 2009, DHS and GSA commenced with construction. DHS and GSA received over a billion dollars with the help of the stimulus act. In classic big-Government style, the bill, intended to help lift America out of the great recession, provided funding for cushy new offices for Washington bureaucrats.

When I say cushy, I am not exaggerating. As our subcommittee Majority staff report from earlier this year showed, the Coast Guard's new headquarters features courtyards built with Brazilian Ipe wood, one of the hardest woods in the world, eco-friendly green roofing, and rain-water flush toilets. These examples illustrate the lack of effective management and oversight of this multibillion-dollar project.

GAO's report lays out in great detail how the St. Elizabeths project has been devoid of leadership and proper management for years. In recent years DHS failed to identify the $4.5 billion project as a major acquisition program within the Department. Such a designation would have brought with it more program oversight. DHS simply can't afford to neglect its oversight responsibilities.

A recent and glaring example of this is a recent inspector general report that showed CBP wasting millions of dollars on lavish housing for employees in Ajo, Arizona. If DHS instilled greater accountability and stricter oversight among its components, millions of dollars in taxpayer dollars could have been saved or put to better use.

Does the fact that these are buildings at St. Elizabeths make a difference and not a Coast Guard ship, a CBP helicopter, or a TSA body scanner? As a result DHS did not require St. Elizabeths to receive the same oversight as other acquisition programs with comparable cost. While doing so may not have solved the problems for the project, they could have given Congress and DHS senior leadership greater visibility on where the program stood.

This mismanagement is exactly why the Senate needs to pass H.R. 4228, the DHS Acquisition Accountability and Efficiency Act, which Mr. Barber, the Ranking Member, and I wrote to increase discipline in DHS acquisitions and ultimately save taxpayer dollars.

GAO also found that DHS and GSA's cost and schedule estimates aren't worth the paper they are printed on. GAO's report shows that the estimates failed to fully comport with any leading capital decision-making practices. Not a one. Consequently, GAO found DHS and GSA's cost and schedule estimates for St. Elizabeths were unreliable and overly optimistic.

It is not a surprise to discover that there has been a wild swing in the estimates since the program has moved forward. In 2007 GSA estimated that the project would be fully complete by 2016 at a cost of $3.2 billion and projected a savings of $743 million by moving employees from leased to owned space. The latest estimates put completion of the project 10 years later, at 2026, and at a cost of $4.5 billion, and reduced savings to $532 million. The truth is DHS and GSA don't have any idea how much St. Elizabeths will cost or when it can be finished.

This is an astounding finding for a program prepared to spend $4.5 billion in taxpayer funds. This lack of basic management, knowing when a project will be done and how much it will cost, is a leadership malpractice. Would any of you sitting at the witness table be willing to commit to building a house with your own money without knowing what it would cost or when it will be done? The answer is no. Yet you expect the American taxpayer to agree to such an ultimatum with St. Elizabeths.

Up until recently DHS and GSA have wanted to continue the course. If you haven't noticed, this Nation is drowning in debt. It has more than doubled from the $8 trillion to over $17 trillion since planning for St. Elizabeths began. Who knows how far in the hole we will be when it is scheduled for completion in 2026. We have serious homeland security priorities that need our attention, such as threats from ISIS and Syrian foreign fighters, foreign fighter flow, dealing with the illegal alien crisis on the Southwest Border, and I could go on and on.

We have had hearings this week in this committee that pointed to where our emphasis needs to be at this time. I commend GAO for its report in shining a light on the mismanagement of St. Elizabeths. Congress should heed GAO's recommendation that no new funding be appropriated until DHS and GSA get their act together. I hope to hear DHS and GSA explain what they plan to do to make this project achievable and affordable, or if that is even possible at this point.

[The statement of Chairman Duncan follows:]

STATEMENT OF CHAIRMAN JEFF DUNCAN

SEPTEMBER 19, 2014

Since 2006, the Department of Homeland Security (DHS) and General Services Administration (GSA) have spent over a billion taxpayer dollars to build a consolidated DHS Headquarters on the St. Elizabeths campus in Southeast Washington, DC. St. Elizabeths is a National historic landmark that was originally founded in 1852 as the Government Hospital for the Insane. The purpose of the new headquarters was to consolidate DHS leadership and operations to improve efficiency. Unfortunately, as shown by a Government Accountability Office (GAO) report that was released today, the project has become a monument to mismanagement.

DHS and GSA spent 3 years planning for the project before 1 ounce of concrete was poured. Finally, in 2009, DHS and GSA commenced with construction. DHS and GSA received over $1 billion with the help of the "Stimulus Act." In classic big-Government style, the bill intended to help lift America out of the "Great Recession" provided funding for cushy new offices for Washington bureaucrats. And when I say cushy, I'm not exaggerating. As our subcommittee Majority staff report from earlier this year showed, the Coast Guard's new headquarters features courtyards built with Brazilian Ipe wood—one of the hardest woods in the world—eco-friendly green roofing and rainwater toilets. These examples illustrate the lack of effective management and oversight of this multibillion-dollar project.

GAO's report lays out in great detail how the St. Elizabeths project has been devoid of leadership and proper management for years. In recent years, DHS failed to identify the $4.5 billion project as a major acquisition program within the Department. Such a designation would have brought with it more program oversight. DHS simply can't afford to neglect its oversight responsibilities. A recent and glaring example of this is a recent inspector general report that showed CBP wasting millions of dollars on lavish housing for employees in Ajo, Arizona. Had DHS instilled greater accountability and stricter oversight among its components, millions of taxpayer dollars could have been saved or put to better use.

Does the fact that these are buildings at St. Elizabeths make a difference and not a Coast Guard ship, CBP helicopter, or TSA body scanner? As a result, DHS did not require St. Elizabeths to receive the same oversight as other acquisition programs with comparable costs. While doing so may not have solved the problems for the project, it could have given Congress and DHS senior leadership greater visibility on where the program stood. This mismanagement is exactly why the Senate needs to pass H.R. 4228—the DHS Acquisition Accountability and Efficiency Act, which Mr. Barber and I wrote to increase discipline in DHS acquisitions and save taxpayer dollars.

GAO also found that DHS and GSA's cost and schedule estimates aren't worth the paper they're printed on. GAO's report shows that the estimates failed to fully comport with any leading capital decision-making practices. Not a one. Consequently, GAO found DHS and GSA's cost and schedule estimates for St. Elizabeths were unreliable and overly optimistic. It's not a surprise to discover that there's been a wild swing in the estimates since the program has moved forward. In 2007, GSA estimated that the project would be fully complete by 2016 at a cost of $3.2 billion and projected a savings of $743 million by moving employees from leased to owned space. The latest estimates put completion of the project at 2026 at a cost of $4.5 billion and reduced savings to $532 million. The truth is that DHS and GSA don't have any idea how much St. Elizabeths will cost or when it could be finished.

This is an astounding finding for a program prepared to spend $4.5 billion in taxpayer funds. This lack of basic management—knowing when a project will be done and how much it will cost—is leadership malpractice. Would any of you sitting at the witness table be willing to commit to building a house with your own money without knowing what it will cost or when it will be done? The answer is: No. Yet, you expect the American taxpayer to agree to such an ultimatum at St. Elizabeths.

Up until recently, DHS and GSA have wanted to continue the course. If you haven't noticed, this Nation is drowning in debt; it's more than doubled from $8 trillion to over $17 trillion since planning for St. Elizabeths began. Who knows how far in the hole we will be when it's scheduled for completion in 2026? And we have serious homeland security priorities that need our attention, such as threats from ISIS and Syrian foreign fighters, the illegal alien crisis on the Southwest Border, and I could go on. I commend GAO for its report and shining a light on the mismanagement of St. Elizabeths. Congress should heed GAO's recommendation that no new funding be appropriated until DHS and GSA get their act together. I hope to hear DHS and GSA explain what they plan to do to make this project achievable and affordable or if that's even possible at this point.

Source: GSA

Source: GAO 14-648

Source: Committee

Source: GSA

Mr. DUNCAN. I will now recognize the Ranking Member of the subcommittee, the gentleman from Arizona, Mr. Barber, for any statement that he may have.

Mr. BARBER. Thank you, Mr. Chairman, and thank you to the witnesses for being with us this morning. Before I give my remarks, Mr. Chairman, I have some additional business to conduct with your approval. I ask unanimous consent for the gentlelady from the District of Columbia to sit in for the purpose of receiving testimony and questioning.

Mr. DUNCAN. Without objection, so ordered.

Mr. BARBER. Additionally, Mr. Chairman, I ask unanimous consent for the report, "Security and Savings: The Importance of Consolidating the Department of Homeland Security's Headquarters at St. Elizabeths," by Senator Tom Carper, to be inserted into the record.

Mr. DUNCAN. Without objection, so ordered.*

Mr. BARBER. Finally, Mr. Chairman, I also ask unanimous consent for the testimony from former Under Secretary for Management Paul A. Schneider to be inserted into the record.

Mr. DUNCAN. Without objection.

[The information follows:]

STATEMENT OF PAUL A. SCHNEIDER, FORMER DEPUTY SECRETARY, DEPARTMENT OF HOMELAND SECURITY

SEPTEMBER 19, 2014

Thank you Chairman Duncan, Ranking Member Barber, and Members of the subcommittee. It's a pleasure to submit this testimony on this very important subject.

It has been approximately 5 years since I have left office as the deputy secretary of the U.S. Department of Homeland Security (DHS) having first served as the under secretary for management. Since that time, I have been consulting for the

_____
*The information has been retained in committee files and is available at *http://hsgac.senate.gov/download/carper-report*.

U.S. Government (except for DHS); am a principal in The Chertoff Group which is a company that provides consulting, security, and merger and acquisition (M&A) advisory services for clients in the security, defense, intelligence, and Government services industries around the world. I also currently serve on several boards and advisory groups, including chairman of the Board of Directors of the Applied Science Foundation for Homeland Security, chairman of the AFCEA Homeland Security Committee, the Naval Studies Board of the National Academy of Sciences and Engineering; and a STRATCOM advisory board for the replacement of the OHIO ballistic missile submarine.

Since leaving my position at DHS, I have had the opportunity to observe the changing and challenging environment and assess its impact on DHS operations and those of the homeland security enterprise. Based on my observations, former position and years of experience, I am here today to provide my views about the importance of consolidating DHS facilities at St. Elizabeths (St. Es).

THE ENVIRONMENT

The homeland security strategic environment is constantly evolving, and while we have made significant progress, threats from terrorism continue to persist. Today's threats are not limited to any one individual or group, are not defined or contained by international borders, and are not limited to any single ideology. Terrorist tactics can be as simple as a home-made bomb and as sophisticated as a biological threat or a coordinated cyber attack. In addition, broader strategic trends such as the dramatic spread of internet and mobile technologies around the world and the growing relevance of non-state actors on the world stage suggest new opportunities and challenges that must be accounted for in our current and longer-term homeland security strategic planning.

Another defining characteristic of our strategic environment is the tightening fiscal environment. It is increasingly important to define clear priorities, develop and assess viable alternatives, and make well-informed decisions involving difficult trade-offs. DHS has made substantial progress in this regard, particularly with respect to establishing a strategic foundation for National homeland security efforts, refining our strategic and policy analysis capabilities and approaches, and improving strategic alignment through focused management tools and processes. Together, these improvements have positioned DHS to effectively address today's security environment while ensuring that we are sufficiently flexible, agile, and capable in the face of emerging threats and risks.

QUADRENNIAL HOMELAND SECURITY REVIEW (QHSR)

Implementing the 9/11 Commission Recommendations Act of 2007 directed the Department to begin conducting quadrennial reviews in 2009 and every 4 years thereafter. The QHSR was a critical first step in the process of examining and addressing fundamental strategic issues that concern homeland security, and establishing an enduring strategic foundation.

As the first review of its kind for DHS, the 2010 QHSR clarified the conceptual underpinnings of homeland security, described the security environment and the Nation's homeland security interests, identified the critical homeland security enterprise missions, and outlined the principal goals and essential objectives necessary for success in those missions.

The 2014 QHSR provides the updated strategy and planning foundation that positions DHS to effectively address the emerging strategic challenges the country faces.

First, the QHSR clarifies the conceptual underpinnings of homeland security. In defining homeland security as the intersection of evolving threats and hazards with traditional Governmental and civic responsibilities for civil defense, emergency response, law enforcement, customs, border control, and immigration. The QHSR emphasizes the importance of eliminating traditional stovepipes to achieving success in homeland security. The QHSR also establishes the idea of the homeland security enterprise which refers to the collective efforts and shared responsibilities of Federal, State, local, Tribal, territorial, non-Governmental, and private-sector partners—as well as individuals, families, and communities—to maintain critical homeland security capabilities. Each of these conceptual elements has infused all aspects strategy and planning.

Second, the QHSR takes a comprehensive approach to threats by expanding the focus of homeland security to specifically address high-consequence weapons of mass destruction, global violent extremism, mass cyber-attacks, intrusions, and disruptions, pandemics and natural disasters, and illegal trafficking and related transnational crime.

Third, the QHSR adopted a mission structure designed to endure across inevitable changes in the security environment. The missions are to prevent terrorism and enhance security, secure and manage our borders, enforce our immigration laws, safeguard and secure cyber space, enhance resilience to disasters, and provide critical support to economic and National security. Because tomorrow's security environment will not necessarily look like today's security environment, the missions provide a durable framework to effectively address whatever risks and threats may emerge over time.

MANAGEMENT CHALLENGE

The Department faces significant management and programmatic challenges. When it was created it was the largest Government reorganization in more than 50 years, involving over 180,000 employees and a budget of more than $40 billion. This effort required the integration of 22 different agencies with different missions, value, cultures, and protocols into a single, unified Department focused on the critical and pressing mission of securing the Nation. Now there are approximately 240,000 people.

Since its formation each Secretary has worked to integrate the various component elements and maximize efficiency, while still keeping the homeland safe and secure. Successful transformations of this sort—even ones less formidable—often take a long time to achieve. DHS must organize around missions, rather than legacy bureaucracies, and it must find ways to resolve old disconnects in its systems. In short, the Department must operate as "One DHS," a unified Department.

Secretary Johnson has developed a strong Strategic Plan to face these challenges and to succeed. His April 2014 memo, "Strengthening the Department Unity of Effort" outlines major management initiatives that are key to the management component that is essential to effectively execute the operational initiatives in the QHSR. It continues along the path to improve operations as "One DHS".

The consolidation of DHS activities at St. Es is an essential element of this transformation and key to the success of several DHS management initiatives.

CONSOLIDATED HEADQUARTERS

DHS's mission demands an integrated approach, yet the Department's legacy facilities are dispersed in more than 50 locations and 7.1 million Gross Square Feet (GSQF) of office space throughout the National Capital Region (NCR). This data may be slightly inaccurate because it is based on my recollection of the situation prior to the United States Coast Guard move. This dispersal adversely impacts critical communication, coordination, and cooperation across the Department. Consolidating executive leadership in a secure setting with sufficient office space for policy, management, operational coordination, and command-and-control capabilities at the St. Elizabeths (St. Es) West Campus is vital to the long-term success of the Department. The Department also needs to reduce the total number of locations that house DHS components in the NCR to as few as possible in order to lower overall costs.

Without Federal construction at St. Es, DHS will continue to be housed in over 50 NCR locations. The St. Es development will result in a $1 billion Net Present Value (NPV) savings over a 30-year period by consolidating private- and public-sector lease agreements. I believe that these estimates that I worked with at the time should be reasonably accurate today.

There are several practical aspects of this matter that I have personally lived through and are as relevant today as they were then.

First, the physical condition of the current DHS Headquarters at Nebraska Ave (called the NAC) is deplorable. In my previous appearances before the Congress I have referred to it as "Dump". It is. The decrepit nature of the physical plant was terrible and in need of constant major maintenance. Maintenance frequently required repeated tearing up the roads and major disruption at the NAC. It was a death spiral, constantly spending money to preserve the old and outdated. Also, several of the operational components were housed in facilities outside the NAC that were inadequate and the habitability was poor.

Second, the space and conditions for a professional workforce was terrible. People crammed into spaces one half or less than the minimum standard by any comparison is unsatisfactory at best. This had an additional flaw in that there was very little open space, hence no flexibility. So, when special task force or teams were required to be formed, the buildings and spaces were not modular and could not be rapidly reconfigured to accommodate the specific mission teams that were required to be established.

Third, actions were taken by previous Congresses to prevent DHS from improving critical operational facilities at the NAC by creating a temporary consolidated operations center, were not allowed (in effect by disapproving financial reprogramming) because the Department would be moving to a consolidated headquarters at St. Es where there would be an integrated operations center. While I found this action unconscionable, I understood it. In my time at the Department, the operations center size was significantly inadequate, the IT technology practically obsolete, and the environment was operational limiting to equipment operational requirements and hence its ability for reliable operations was severely impacted. A major consideration in the design of the St. Es campus was the establishment of the integrated operations center; specifically to exercise the required leadership and direction of the operations. The failure to accomplish this is unacceptable from a security standpoint.

Fourth, the wide-spread dispersal of the operational component's key leadership made leadership and command and control very difficult. Trying to gather the operational leadership in times where joint operations are required to focus on emergent crises is near impossible given the current geographic dispersal. In this regard, what is often overlooked by those outside the Department is that DHS is a huge operational law enforcement organization. Co-location of the leadership to exercise direction of operations is an essential aspect of good command and control. It would be unthinkable for any law enforcement organization of substantially less size to be forced to operate in a manner similar to the current DHS layout, yet it is tolerated and accepted for DHS which was established to provide enhanced and integrated security operations to protect the homeland. This is not a mere dollars issue. Failure to enable the consolidation is operational limiting.

Fifth, in the D.C. area, if there is an emergency homeland security event, the activity dispersal will essentially preclude assembling the leadership because the major traffic disruption that will probably result will make movement across the city impossible.

Sixth, the many leases and rents for DHS organizations outside of the District of Columbia. While in office I was frequently asked by Members and staff why can't you consolidate disparate DHS activity locations across the country. Practically we started to do that where it made sense and where timing of expired leases could be synchronized to avoid penalties. In all these discussions I expressed my concern that while these efforts were important, they were indeed very minor compared to the challenges and opportunities faced in the District of Columbia.

Seventh, the consolidation of mission support functions that cannot be accommodated at St. Es also has the potential to achieve comparable cost avoidances through co-location of similar functions, elimination of redundancies, and economize shared services. It was always recognized that there were efficiencies that could be achieved in consolidating several of these "back room" functions, mostly administrative that were more site-independent than operationally-focused and co-location required. Our plan was simple—co-locate the operational leadership and then look to consolidate the back room functions. That plan made sense in 2009 and it makes sense today.

This effort will right-size the real estate portfolio resulting in DHS having 70 percent of its offices in less costly yet more secure Government-owned space.

Consolidating facilities will increase efficiency, enhance communication, and foster a "One DHS" culture that will optimize Department-wide prevention and response capability. I strongly request that the Congress support this effort by authorizing and appropriating funding for completing the DHS consolidation at St. Elizabeths West Campus and efficient realignment of off-campus locations.

CONCLUSION

Thank you for your leadership and your continued support of the Department of Homeland Security and its important programs and your efforts in shaping the future and success of DHS. I sincerely appreciate this opportunity to submit this testimony for the record in support of the consolidation of DHS activities at St. Es.

Mr. BARBER. Well, thank you, Mr. Chairman, and thank you for convening this hearing this morning. You will recall that you and I went out to St. Elizabeths several months ago to see what was going on and what was in progress, and at that time none of the buildings were completed. We were still waiting for the first one to be opened and occupied. That has now happened with the Coast Guard moving from the Navy Yard into St. Elizabeths. I have not been out there since, but I hope when we return to pay another visit to see what other progress has been made.

As we know, the Department of Homeland Security is composed of 22 sometimes called legacy agencies, making it the third-largest department in the Federal Government. It has, I believe, one of the most important missions of any Federal agency, and that is to keep Americans safe and to protect the homeland. This is an enormous challenge and responsibility from securing our borders to counter-terrorism and cybersecurity.

In 2006, former DHS Secretary Michael Chertoff introduced a plan to consolidate the Department's senior leadership across all 22 component agencies into one headquarters, as opposed to operating out of 50 different locations around the Nation's Capital Region. In the consolidated headquarters, the Department would be in one location and could more quickly coordinate and respond to a crisis. As we know, St. Elizabeths Hospital in Southeast Washington was chosen as the site for this consolidation plan.

The original master plan for converting St. Elizabeths into a DHS Headquarters called for a coordinated construction schedule that would be divided into three phases, and it was supposed to cost $3.45 billion with the project being completed by 2015, next year. Unfortunately, Mr. Chairman, as you pointed out, the project is now expected to exceed costs of $4.5 billion. It is now expected to be completed in 2026. That is a $1 billion increase in cost projections and 11 years overdue.

There are several issues, as we know, behind the costs and the delays that St. Elizabeths is experiencing, and I am looking forward to an opportunity today to explore further those issues and those delays.

First, the GAO found that in managing this project the Department of Homeland Security and the General Services Administration did not fully conform with leading capital decision-making practices. The GAO also found that DHS and GSA have not conducted an assessment of current needs and capability gaps, nor have they prioritized alternative designs that would help adapt St. Elizabeths' consolidation plan to meet the current fiscal environment.

Another issue that has plagued St. Elizabeths is a funding gap that began in the first year after the first phase of construction. In fiscal 2006 President Bush requested almost $38 million to begin the first phase of construction specifically for consolidating the Coast Guard at St. Elizabeths and to upgrade St. Elizabeths' West Campus infrastructure, and Congress fully funded this request. However, in fiscal year 2007, when President Bush requested roughly $360 million for St. Elizabeths, Congress only appropriated about $6 million, creating a significant funding gap. The funding gap has widened over the years and has contributed to project delays and to cost inflations.

As Ranking Member of this subcommittee, I am committed to working with my colleagues on both sides of the aisle to ensure that the Department spends taxpayer money wisely. We have to be good fiscal agents. The Department must have the resources it needs to fulfill its mission, but we will not and should not write them a blank check. They must accord to best practices and have plans in place that enable them to adapt to the current fiscal and legislative climate.

Let me just digress for a moment, Mr. Chairman, to point out that this is not just an issue at St. Elizabeths. Recently, there was a report that showed in my State, in the district next door, another cost overrun in an inexplicable building project, building houses for Border Patrol Agents and their families in a small community called Ajo. It used to be a mining town. It is now essentially a retirement community. The home values in Ajo are about $88,000 on the average. What did DHS spend with GSA to build those homes? Almost $700,000 per home, building homes that were larger than were needed for agents whose families were living in Tucson and other cities who were not likely to occupy the larger premises.

Earlier this year we heard another GAO report that pointed out a $24 million boondoggle, I might say, which was an effort to upgrade the IT system for DHS. That plan was never implemented because the implementation or the proposal was not appropriate to the need.

So today's hearing will obviously focus on St. Elizabeths, but I think we have to be concerned about a broader problem, and that is how does this third-largest Federal agency manage the money that the taxpayers give to us and we to them to fund the agency's mission? I also look forward to hearing from GSA and DHS about why the consolidation plan is important to protecting our homeland and whether or not one location is financially more practical than the Department's current leasing system.

Let me, Mr. Chairman, close with this remark. I have been very impressed, as I think we have on both sides of the aisle in this committee, with Secretary Johnson's commitment to transparency and accountability. I understand that he will be looking at these issues very seriously and I believe he will take action. I look forward to his action being one that is good for the taxpayer and gets these projects done on time and on budget.

Thank you, Mr. Chairman. I yield back.

[The statement of Ranking Member Barber follows:]

STATEMENT OF RANKING MEMBER RON BARBER

SEPTEMBER 19, 2014

The Department of Homeland Security is made up of 22 legacy agencies, making it the third-largest department in the Federal Government. DHS has one of the most important missions of our Government—to keep Americans safe. This is an enormous challenge and responsibility, from securing our borders, to counterterrorism and cybersecurity. In 2006, former DHS Secretary Michael Chertoff introduced a plan to consolidate the Department's senior leadership—across all 22 component agencies—into one headquarters.

As opposed to operating out of 50 different locations around the National Capital Region, in a consolidated headquarters the Department would be in one location and could quickly coordinate and respond to a crisis.

As we know, the site selected for this consolidation plan was St. Elizabeths Hospital in Southeast Washington. The original master plan for St. Elizabeths called for a coordinated construction schedule to be divided into three phases and to cost $3.45 billion, with the project being completed by 2015.

Unfortunately, the project is now expected to cost $4.5 billion and is not expected to be completed until 2026. There are several issues behind the costs and delay at St. Elizabeths that I am hoping we can explore further through today's hearing.

First, the Government Accountability Office found that in managing this project the Department of Homeland Security and the General Services Administration did not fully conform with leading capital decision-making practices. The GAO also found that DHS and GSA have not conducted an assessment of current needs and capability gaps, nor have they prioritized alternative designs that would help adapt the St. Elizabeths consolidation plan to meet the current fiscal environment.

Another issue that has plagued St. Elizabeths is a funding gap that began in just a year after the first phase of construction. In fiscal year 2006, President Bush requested almost $38 million to begin the first phase of construction, specifically for consolidating the Coast Guard at St. Elizabeths and to upgrade St. Elizabeths West Campus infrastructure. Congress fully funded this request.

However, in fiscal year 2007, when President Bush requested roughly $360 million for St. Elizabeths, Congress only appropriated around $6 million. The funding gap has widened over the years and has contributed to project delays and to cost inflations.

As Ranking Member of this subcommittee, I am committed to working with my colleagues on both sides of the aisle to ensure that the Department spends taxpayer dollars wisely. The Department must have the resources they need to fulfill their mission but we will not write them a blank check. They must accord to best practices and have plans in place that enable them to adapt to the current fiscal and legislative climate.

Today's hearing should provide an opportunity to hear from GAO regarding its analysis of the St. Elizabeths project and its recommendations to GSA and DHS. I also look forward to hearing from GSA and DHS about why the consolidation plan is important to protecting our homeland and whether or not one location is financially more practical than the Department's current leasing system.

Mr. DUNCAN. I thank the gentleman.

Other Members of the subcommittee are reminded that opening statements may be submitted for the record.

[The statement of Ranking Member Thompson follows:]

STATEMENT OF RANKING MEMBER BENNIE G. THOMPSON

SEPTEMBER 19, 2014

Since the Department of Homeland Security was created in 2002, its core components have been dispersed in more than 50 locations throughout the National Capital Region. This separation adversely affects the need for cohesive communication, coordination, and cooperation across the Department component agencies as the Department seeks to fulfill its mission.

At a time when we face a dynamic threat picture and realize a natural disaster could occur in any area of the country, it is inconceivable that the Department of Homeland Security does not have a consolidated headquarters where the Secretary can meet with the component heads instantaneously.

Secretary Johnson has indicated his vision to unify the Department, and Members of this committee have vocally supported him; however, we must recognize that having the Department spread throughout the National Capital Region has a negative impact on the Secretary's vision. Former Secretary Chertoff presented the plan to have a single, unified headquarters that houses the Secretary, senior Department leadership, and component heads at the St. Elizabeths West campus in southeast DC.

I was a vocal supporter of the DHS consolidation plan when it was first presented. At that time, I expressed my concerns about the Department and its track record of taking on large-scale procurement projects. I also asked DHS and GSA to make sure that small and minority businesses were a part of the fabric of this consolidation. DHS and GSA completed the first phase of the three-phase consolidation project on time and on budget.

However, Phase II and III of the consolidation project have been stalled. According to the Government Accountability Office, St. Elizabeths lacks reliable cost and schedule estimating practices. However, we must look at what DHS and GSA have to work with. The DHS consolidation plan has never been has not received full funding for the headquarters consolidation since the American Recovery and Reinvestment Act (ARRA) funding was appropriated in fiscal years 2009 to 2010 which allowed for the U.S. Coast Guard Headquarters to be completed during Phase I of the construction.

As we are here to look at GAO and its audit, we must recognize everyone's responsibility in this matter. GSA serves as the broker, developer, and property manager for the headquarters consolidation. However, Congressional appropriation of funding of St. Elizabeths continues to be uncertain as the House's fiscal year 2015 Financial Service and General Government Appropriations bill zeroed out funding for GSA.

How can we expect the Department to have a consolidated headquarters if we do not give them money to build it? Mr. Chairman, as we are here to examine waste, fraud, and abuse—let's keep some common-sense and figures in mind—if the consolidation project was completed, the Federal Government would own the space. Sixty-nine percent of the commercial leases for DHS will expire between fiscal years 2016 and 2020.

The headquarters consolidation is $4.5 billion, DHS would spend upwards of $5.2 billion, or approximately $700 million more over the next 30 years to continue leasing space in the National Capital Region. St. Elizabeths will cost the Department more up-front, but over time, the headquarters consolidation will pay for itself as its tenant costs will only be competed once. In an era where we daily speak about waste, fraud, and abuse, we should be vigilant and understand the costs of this project and take steps to fund it.

Mr. DUNCAN. We are pleased to have a distinguished panel of witnesses before us today on this important topic. Let me remind the witnesses that their entire written statement will appear in the record. I will introduce each of you first and then I will recognize you individually for your testimony.

Our first witness is Mr. David Maurer. He became the director in the Government Accountability Office, GAO, Homeland Security and Justice team in 2009, where he leads GAO's work reviewing DHS and DOJ management issues. His work recently covers DHS management integration, nuclear smuggling, research and development at DHS, DOJ grant management, crowding in the Federal prison system, and counterterrorism staffing vacancies at the FBI.

The second witness is Mr. Chris Cummiskey. He was appointed acting under secretary for management at DHS earlier this year. Mr. Cummiskey oversees Management Directorate's programs, processes, and personnel through the six line business chiefs. The director is responsible for Department-wide management and operations. Mr. Cummiskey also serves as the chief acquisition officer, overseeing $19 billion in acquisition programs and overseeing the Department's headquarter consolidation project at St. Elizabeths. Prior to his appointment to this position, he served as deputy under secretary for management and chief of staff for the Management Directorate.

Our third witness is Mr. Norman Dong. He serves as the commissioner of the Public Buildings Service for the USGSA. Through this position, Mr. Dong leads one of the largest and most diversified public real estate portfolios in the world, managing Nationwide assets, design, construction, leasing, building management, and disposal of Federal building space. Prior to joining GSA, Mr. Dong was acting controller at the Office of Management and Budget.

I want to thank all of you gentlemen for being here today. I will now recognize Mr. Maurer to testify.

STATEMENT OF DAVID C. MAURER, DIRECTOR, HOMELAND SECURITY AND JUSTICE, U.S. GOVERNMENT ACCOUNTABILITY OFFICE

Mr. MAURER. Good morning, Chairman Duncan, Ranking Member Barber, and other Members and staff. I am pleased to be here today to discuss the findings from our review of DHS Headquarters consolidation at the St. Elizabeths campus here in the District of Columbia.

This is not a new issue. Seven years ago we issued a report expressing concerns about the future of the project. We recommended, among other things, that GSA and DHS develop a comprehensive cost analysis and comparison of alternatives. Both DHS and GSA said a dispersed DHS Headquarters was unacceptable and did not see the need to further refine estimates or consider alternatives. That proved to be a missed opportunity. So here we are today, costs have grown, schedules have slipped, and we are now, under current plans, 12 years away from project completion.

Now, it is important to recognize that GAO has no position on whether DHS should consolidate its headquarters at St. Elizabeths. That is a policy call. Congress will ultimately decide what to fund and when to fund it. Our report being issued today is designed to help inform those decisions.

We do think it is critically important for DHS and GSA to update plans, adapt to a change in circumstances, and apply leading practices. Our work found significant problems in the current plans and cost and schedule estimates.

DHS and GSA issued the current plans in a series of documents from 2006 through 2009. Unfortunately, these plans are frozen in time. A lot has changed. Congress has provided $1.6 billion less in funding than requested. DHS' footprint in the National Capital Region has grown over 20 percent. Standards for telework and average space per worker have changed. DHS and GSA need to update their plans to reflect these realities.

More fundamentally, it is worth taking an updated look at alternative approaches to headquarters consolidation to ensure building out St. Elizabeths is the best, most cost-efficient option for meeting DHS' needs. That would include reviewing, among other things, DHS' current National Capital Region leasing portfolio.

We also reviewed the current cost estimates for the project and found that they are unreliable because, at best, they only partially conform to leading practices. For example, DHS and GSA have not regularly updated their estimates and have optimistically assumed future cost growth no greater than the rate of inflation. We also found that the project schedule only minimally conforms to leading practices. Among other things, it does not fully account for when labor, material, and equipment will be needed and has not been fully updated since 2008.

GSA contends their leading practices don't apply to large-scale construction projects like St. Elizabeths. We think they do. In fact, GSA was involved in developing our leading practices. They are recognized and required by OMB and have been used to assess several construction projects at a wide variety of Federal agencies. But to be fair, at GSA's request, we did additional work looking at their compliance with their own standards for cost and schedule. We found that all too often GSA did not comply with its own rules.

For example, GSA guidance requires projects to develop a life-cycle cost estimate that includes the cost to build and operate the facility. However, the St. Elizabeths cost estimate only includes the cost to build, not the cost of repair, operations, and maintenance. GSA guidance calls for developing an approved baseline schedule to allow comparison between planned and actual time frames. We found no evidence of a schedule baseline document to help measure performance of the project.

We have recommendations in our report to strengthen the management of this project, and I am pleased that DHS and GSA agree with them and will be updating their plans, improving their oversight, and enhancing their cost and schedule estimates. That is a big improvement over 7 years ago. It will help enhance the overall management of this large, complex project and provide Congress better information to inform future decisions.

In closing, Congress needs a clearer road map for the St. Elizabeths project. You need to know how long it will take, how much it will cost, and how it will ultimately benefit the taxpayers. Our report concludes that Congress should consider making future funding for St. Elizabeths contingent on DHS and GSA answering those questions. Implementing our recommendations will better position both organizations to do just that.

That concludes my opening remarks. Thank you for the opportunity to testify this morning.

[The prepared statement of Mr. Maurer follows:]

PREPARED STATEMENT OF DAVID C. MAURER

SEPTEMBER 19, 2014

Mr. Chairman and Members of the subcommittee: I am pleased to be here today to discuss our report, which is being released today, on the Department of Homeland Security (DHS) Headquarters consolidation project at St. Elizabeths Campus in Washington, DC.[1] The $4.5 billion construction project, managed by DHS and the General Services Administration (GSA),[2] is the centerpiece of DHS's larger effort to manage and consolidate its workforce of over 20,000 in the National Capital Region (NCR).[3] As conceived in 2006, the Federally-owned St. Elizabeths site was designed to consolidate DHS's executive leadership, operational management, and other personnel at one secure location rather than at multiple locations throughout the Washington, DC, metropolitan area.[4] Specifically, DHS envisioned moving about 14,000 staff to the new headquarters facility and housing its remaining personnel in other consolidated spaces across the region. With a current projected completion date of 2026, the St. Elizabeths project is intended to provide DHS a secure facility to allow for more efficient incident management response and command-and-control operations, and also provide long-term cost savings by reducing reliance on leased space.

My testimony is based on and summarizes the key findings of our report issued today, on DHS and GSA efforts to manage the DHS headquarter consolidation project. My statement will address the extent to which DHS and GSA have: (1) Developed DHS Headquarters consolidation plans in accordance with leading capital decision-making practices and (2) estimated the costs and schedules of the DHS Headquarters consolidation project at St. Elizabeths in a manner that is consistent with leading practices. To do our work we compared DHS and GSA capital planning efforts against applicable leading practices in capital decision making and interviewed DHS and GSA officials responsible for the planning and management of the

---

[1] GAO, *Federal Real Property: DHS and GSA Need to Strengthen the Management of DHS Headquarters Consolidation*, GAO–14–648 (Washington, DC: Sept. 19, 2014).

[2] GSA, the landlord for the civilian Federal Government, acquires space on behalf of the Federal Government through new construction and leasing, and acts as a caretaker for Federal properties across the country. As such, GSA had the responsibility to select the specific site for a new, consolidated DHS Headquarters facility, based on DHS needs and requirements.

[3] The National Capital Region is composed of the District of Columbia and nearby jurisdictions in Maryland and Virginia.

[4] The St. Elizabeths campus is a National Historic Landmark and a former Federally-run hospital for the mentally ill.

DHS Headquarters consolidation.[5] We also compared DHS and GSA documents on the estimated cost and schedule for the St. Elizabeths project with GAO cost- and schedule-estimating leading practices and relevant GSA guidance.[6] More detailed information on the scope and methodology can be found in our published report.[7] The work upon which this statement is based was conducted in accordance with generally accepted Government auditing standards.

BACKGROUND

The Homeland Security Act of 2002 combined 22 Federal agencies specializing in various missions under DHS.[8] Numerous Departmental offices and seven key operating components are headquartered in the NCR.[9] When DHS was formed, the headquarters functions of its various components were not physically consolidated, but instead were dispersed across the NCR in accordance with their history. As of July 2014, DHS employees were located in 94 buildings and 50 locations, accounting for approximately 9 million gross square feet of Government-owned and -leased office space.

DHS began planning the consolidation of its headquarters in 2005. According to DHS, increased colocation and consolidation were critical to: (1) Improve mission effectiveness, (2) create a unified DHS organization, (3) increase organizational efficiency, (4) size the real estate portfolio accurately to fit the mission of DHS, and (5) reduce real estate occupancy costs. Between 2006 and 2009, DHS and GSA developed a number of capital planning documents to guide the DHS Headquarters consolidation process. For example, DHS's National Capital Region Housing Master Plan identified a requirement for approximately 4.5 million square feet of office space on a secure campus. In addition, DHS's 2007 Consolidated Headquarters Collocation Plan summarized component functional requirements and the projected number of seats needed on- and off-campus for NCR Headquarters personnel.

From fiscal year 2006 through fiscal year 2014, the St. Elizabeths consolidation project had received $494.8 million through DHS appropriations and $1.1 billion through GSA appropriations, for a total of over $1.5 billion. However, from fiscal year 2009—when construction began—through the time of the fiscal year 2014 appropriation, the gap between requested and received funding was over $1.6 billion. According to DHS and GSA officials, this gap created cost escalations of over $1 billion and schedule delays of over 10 years.

DHS AND GSA CONSOLIDATION PLANS DID NOT FULLY CONFORM WITH LEADING CAPITAL DECISION-MAKING PRACTICES

In our September 2014 report, we found that DHS and GSA planning for the DHS Headquarters consolidation did not fully conform with leading capital decision-making practices intended to help agencies effectively plan and procure assets.[10] Specifically, we found that DHS and GSA had not conducted a comprehensive assessment of current needs, identified capability gaps, or evaluated and prioritized alternatives that would help officials adapt consolidation plans to changing conditions and address funding issues as reflected in leading practices. DHS and GSA officials reported that they had taken some initial actions that may facilitate consolidation planning in a manner consistent with leading practices. For example, DHS has an overall goal of reducing the square footage allotted per employee across the Depart-

---

[5] GAO, *Executive Guide: Leading Practices in Capital Decision-Making*; GAO/AIMD–99–32 (Washington, DC: Dec. 1, 1998) and Office of Management and Budget (OMB), Capital Programming Guide, Supplement to OMB Circular A–11 (Washington, DC: July 2014).

[6] GAO, *GAO Cost Estimating and Assessment Guide: Best Practices for Developing and Managing Capital Program Costs*, GAO–09–3SP (Washington, DC: Mar. 2, 2009) and *GAO Schedule Assessment Guide: Best Practices for Project Schedules*, GAO–12–120G (Washington, DC: May 2012).

[7] GAO–14–648.

[8] Pub. L. No. 107–296, 116 Stat. 2135.

[9] Departmental offices encompass core management and policy functions, among other things. The seven core DHS operating components headquartered in the NCR are U.S. Citizenship and Immigration Services, U.S. Coast Guard, U.S. Customs and Border Protection, Federal Emergency Management Agency, U.S. Immigration and Customs Enforcement, U.S. Secret Service, and Transportation Security Administration.

[10] Congress, OMB, and GAO have all identified the need for effective capital decision making among Federal agencies. OMB's *Capital Programming Guide,* along with GAO's *Executive Guide: Leading Practices in Capital Decision-Making* provides detailed guidance to Federal agencies on leading practices for the four phases of capital programming—planning, budgeting, acquiring, and managing capital assets. These practices are, in part, intended to provide a disciplined approach or process to help Federal agencies effectively plan and procure assets to achieve the maximum return on investment.

ment in accordance with current workplace standards, such as standards for telework and hoteling.[11] DHS and GSA officials acknowledged that new workplace standards could create a number of new development options to consider, as the new standards would allow for more staff to occupy the current space at St. Elizabeths than previously anticipated. DHS and GSA officials also reported analyzing different leasing options that could affect consolidation efforts. However, we found that the consolidation plans, which were finalized between 2006 and 2009, had not been updated to reflect these actions.

In addition, we found that current funding for the St. Elizabeths project had not aligned with what DHS and GSA initially planned. According to DHS and GSA officials, the funding gap between what DHS and GSA requested and what was received from fiscal years 2009 through 2014, was over $1.6 billion. According to these officials, this gap created cost escalations of over $1 billion and schedule delays of over 10 years relative to original estimates. These delays have posed challenges for DHS in terms of its current leasing portfolio. Specifically, DHS's long-term leasing portfolio was developed based on the original expected completion date for St. Elizabeths development in 2016. According to DHS leasing data, 52 percent of DHS's current NCR leases will expire in 2014 and 2015, accounting for almost 39 percent of its usable square feet. However, we found that DHS and GSA had not conducted a comprehensive assessment of current needs, identified capability gaps, or evaluated and prioritized alternatives that would help officials adapt consolidation plans to changing conditions and address funding issues, as reflected in leading practices for capital decision making.[12] DHS and GSA reported that they have begun to work together to consider changes to the DHS Headquarters consolidation plans, but they had not announced when new plans will be issued. Furthermore, because final documentation of agency deliberations or analyses had not yet been developed, it was unclear if any new plans would be informed by an updated comprehensive needs assessment and capability gap analysis as called for by leading capital decision-making practices. Therefore, in our September 2014 report, we recommended that DHS and GSA conduct: (1) A comprehensive needs assessment and gap analysis of current and needed capabilities that takes into consideration changing conditions, and (2) an alternatives analysis that identifies the costs and benefits of leasing and construction alternatives for the remainder of the project and prioritizes options to account for funding instability. DHS and GSA concurred with these recommendations and stated that their forthcoming draft St. Elizabeths Enhanced Consolidation Plan would contain these analyses.

Finally, we found that DHS had not consistently applied its major acquisition guidance for reviewing and approving the headquarters consolidation project. Specifically, we found that DHS had guidelines in place to provide senior management the opportunity to review and approve its major projects, but DHS had not consistently applied these guidelines to its efforts to work with GSA to plan and implement headquarters consolidation. DHS had designated the headquarters consolidation project as a major acquisition in some years but not in others. In 2010 and 2011, DHS identified the headquarters consolidation project as a major acquisition and included the project on DHS's Major Acquisitions Oversight List.[13] Thus, the project was subject to the oversight and management policies and procedures established in DHS major acquisition guidance; however, the project did not comply with major acquisition requirements as outlined by DHS guidelines. For example, we found that the project had not produced any of the required key acquisition documents requiring Department-level approval, such as life-cycle cost estimates and an acquisition program baseline, among others. In 2012, the project as a whole was dropped from the list. In 2013 and 2014, DHS included the information technology (IT) acquisition portion of the project on the list, but not the entire project. DHS officials explained that they considered the St. Elizabeths project to be more of a GSA acquisition than a DHS acquisition because GSA owns the site and the majority of building construction is funded through GSA appropriations. We recognize that GSA has responsibility for managing contracts associated with the headquarters consolidation project.

---

[11] Telework is a work arrangement in which employees perform all or a portion of their work at an alternative work site, such as from home or a telework center. Hoteling allows allow employees to work at multiple sites and use nondedicated, nonpermanent workspaces assigned for use by reservation on an as-needed basis.

[12] GAO/AIMD–99–32 and OMB *Capital Programming Guide.*

[13] DHS reviews its acquisition portfolio annually and designates programs as major acquisitions based on DHS investment thresholds. Generally, programs that incur costs greater than $300 million over the life cycle of the program are considered major acquisitions. In 2014, DHS changed the name of the Major Acquisition Oversight List to the Master Acquisition Oversight List to more accurately distinguish between the Department's major (Level 1 and 2) and non-major (Level 3) acquisitions and non-acquisition activities included in the list.

However, a variety of factors, including the overall cost, scope, and visibility of the project, as well as the overall importance of the project in the context of DHS's mission, make the consolidation project a viable candidate for consideration as a major acquisition. By not consistently applying this review process to headquarters consolidation, we concluded that DHS management risked losing insight into the progress of the St. Elizabeths project, as well as how the project fits in with its overall acquisitions portfolio. Thus, in our September 2014 report, we recommended that the Secretary of Homeland Security designate the headquarters consolidation program a major acquisition, consistent with DHS acquisition policy, and apply DHS acquisition policy requirements. DHS concurred with the recommendation.

DHS AND GSA COST AND SCHEDULE ESTIMATES FOR THE ST. ELIZABETHS PROJECT DID NOT REFLECT LEADING PRACTICES

In our September 2014 report, we found that DHS and GSA cost and schedule estimates for the headquarters consolidation project at St. Elizabeths did not conform or only minimally or partially conformed with leading estimating practices, and were therefore unreliable.[14] Furthermore, we found that in some areas, the cost and schedule estimates did not fully conform with GSA guidance relevant to developing estimates.

Cost Estimates

We found that DHS and GSA cost estimates for the headquarters consolidation project at St. Elizabeths did not reflect leading practices, which rendered the estimates unreliable. For example, we found that the 2013 cost estimate—the most recent available—did not include: (1) A life-cycle cost analysis of the project, including the cost of repair, operations, and maintenance; (2) was not regularly updated to reflect significant changes to the program including actual costs; and (3) did not include an independent estimate to assist in tracking the budget. In addition, a sensitivity analysis had not been performed to assess the reasonableness of the cost estimate. We have previously reported that a reliable cost estimate is critical to the success of any program.[15] Specifically, we have found that such an estimate provides the basis for informed investment decision making, realistic budget formulation and program resourcing, meaningful progress measurement, pro-active course correction when warranted, and accountability for results. Accordingly, we concluded that DHS and GSA would benefit from maintaining current and well-documented estimates of project costs at St. Elizabeths—even if project funding is not fully secured—and these estimates should encompass the full life-cycle of the program and be independently assessed.

Schedule Estimates

In addition, we found that the 2008 and 2013 schedule estimates did not include all activities for both the Government and its contractors necessary to accomplish the project's objectives and did not include schedule baseline documents to help measure performance as reflected in leading practices and GSA guidance. For the 2008 schedule estimate, we also found that resources (such as labor, materials, and equipment) were not accounted for and a risk assessment had not been conducted to predict a level of confidence in the project's completion date. In addition, we found the 2013 schedule estimate was unreliable because, among other things, it was incomplete in that it did not provide details needed to understand the sequence of events, including work to be performed in fiscal years 2014 and 2015.

We concluded that developing cost and schedule estimates consistent with leading practices could promote greater transparency and provide decision makers needed information about the St. Elizabeths project and the larger DHS Headquarters consolidation effort. However, in commenting on our analysis of St. Elizabeths cost and schedule estimates, DHS and GSA officials said that it would be difficult or impossible to create reliable estimates that encompass the scope of the entire St. Elizabeths project. Officials said that given the complex, multi-phase nature of the overall development effort, specific estimates are created for smaller individual projects, but not for the campus project as a whole. Therefore, in their view, leading estimating practices and GSA guidance cannot reasonably be applied to the high-level

---

[14] GAO–09–3SP and GAO–12–120G. For both the cost and schedule estimates, our analysis focused on how well DHS and GSA met each of the four characteristics based on our assessment of conformance to the leading practices associated with that characteristic. We then arrayed the extent to which DHS and GSA cost and schedule estimates conformed with the four characteristics of each using five rating categories—fully meets, substantially meets, partially meets, minimally meets, or does not meet.

[15] GAO–09–3SP.

projections developed for the total cost and completion date of the entire St. Elizabeths project. GSA stated that the higher-level, milestone schedule currently being used to manage the program is more flexible than the detailed schedule GAO proposes, and has proven effective even with the highly-variable funding provided for the project.

We found in our September 2014 report, however, that this high-level schedule was not sufficiently defined to effectively manage the program. For example, our review showed that the schedule did not contain detailed schedule activities that include current Government, contractor, and applicable subcontractor effort. Specifically, the activities shown in the schedule only address high-level agency square footage segments, security, utilities, landscape, and road improvements. While we understand the need to keep future effort contained in high-level planning packages, in accordance with leading practices, near-term work occurring in fiscal years 2014 and 2015 should have more detailed information. We recognize the challenges of developing reliable cost and schedule estimates for a large-scale, multi-phase project like St. Elizabeths, particularly given its unstable funding history and that incorporating GAO's cost- and schedule-estimating leading practices may involve additional costs. However, unless DHS and GSA invest in these practices, Congress risks making funding decisions and DHS and GSA management risk making resource allocation decisions without the benefit that a robust analysis of levels of risk, uncertainty, and confidence provides. As a result, in our September 2014 report, we recommended that, after revising the DHS Headquarters consolidation plans, DHS and GSA develop revised cost and schedule estimates for the remaining portions of the consolidation project that conform to GSA guidance and leading practices for cost and schedule estimation, including an independent evaluation of the estimates. DHS and GSA concurred with the recommendation.

In our September 2014 report, we also stated that Congress should consider making future funding for the St. Elizabeths project contingent upon DHS and GSA developing a revised headquarters consolidation plan, for the remainder of the project, that conforms with leading practices and that: (1) Recognizes changes in workplace standards, (2) identifies which components are to be colocated at St. Elizabeths and in leased and owned space throughout the NCR, and (3) develops and provides reliable cost and schedule estimates.

Mr. Chairman and Members of the subcommittee, this concludes my prepared statement. I look forward to responding to any questions that you may have.

Mr. DUNCAN. Thank you, Mr. Maurer.

The Chairman will now recognize Mr. Cummiskey to testify for 5 minutes.

STATEMENT OF CHRIS CUMMISKEY, ACTING UNDER SECRETARY, MANAGEMENT DIRECTORATE, U.S. DEPARTMENT OF HOMELAND SECURITY

Mr. CUMMISKEY. Good morning, Mr. Chairman and Ranking Member Barber, Members of the committee. Thank you so much for the opportunity to join you this morning. As was indicated, my name is Chris Cummiskey. I am the acting under secretary for management and chief acquisition officer for the Department. It is an opportunity today to share the dais here with Mr. Dong and Mr. Maurer, two gentlemen for which I have utmost respect who have made significant contributions to this project and others.

I appreciate the Chairman and the Ranking Member's efforts certainly around 4228 and other efforts to strengthen acquisition oversight at the Department. We support those efforts and hope that that will pass shortly. I wanted to draw your attention to just a couple of points about the track record of success in the development of St. Elizabeths to date in Phase I, the Coast Guard Headquarters. I also want to assert that through the program of record that we have put on the table taxpayers will save money and will foster greater unity of efforts at the Department.

I have to be honest with you. When I arrived at the Department as part as Secretary Napolitano's team in 2009 as a former State senator and member of the Appropriations Committee there in that State, I had a fair amount of skepticism as to what we had inherited from Secretary Chertoff and his team, but it didn't take long to understand exactly what they were talking about. I think that is reflected in former Deputy Secretary Schneider's comments in that the essential value of this project is the consolidation of the 50 locations across the Department down to something lower than 10, which I think is a critical part of this.

To frame the discussion today, I think it is also important to understand the respective roles and the responsibilities between DHS as a tenant agency and GSA as a landlord. Our role at the Department is to establish program requirements while our partners at GSA manage the property development itself. In fact, the bulk of the funding does go to GSA, and in fiscal year 2014 our share of the money that was appropriated by Congress is $35 million. Our request in fiscal year 2015 is $57 million.

I would just like to make three simple points. The first thing I want to draw your attention to is the record of success in what we delivered with the Coast Guard Headquarters at St. Elizabeths. That project, for the portions that were funded by Congress, came in on time and on budget for the moneys that Chairman Duncan articulated. When we receive consistent funding, we can deliver on time and on budget. We have accomplished that and we believe that can be accomplished through the remainder of the phases.

Second, I want to highlight the benefits to the U.S. taxpayer of continued consolidation of the DHS footprint. In the 2013 review of GSA high-value leases, GAO noted the timing is ripe for targeted investments to take the Department out of long-term, high-value commercial leases and into efficient Federally-owned space and lower long-term costs. With 69 percent of DHS' Headquarters and component leases in the NCR expiring between fiscal year 2016 and fiscal year 2020, the Department will pay for those replacements regardless of the future of St. Elizabeths funding. By consolidating our operations at St. Elizabeths, the 30-year present value cost of Federal construction is nearly $700 million less than commercial leasing as reported by GSA, in their fiscal year 2015 prospectus submission, indicates.

Third, headquarters consolidation enhances the Unity of Effort that Secretary Johnson has so articulately depicted at DHS. A key focus for the Secretary has been to bring together the disparate components that are spread across the NCR, and after 6 years at the Department I have seen first-hand what it means when you are in a crisis situation and your component heads are scattered across the National Capital Region.

One of the things that this project brings to bear is the centralization of The National Operations Center, which Secretary Chertoff and Deputy Secretary Schneider and so many of my former colleagues have articulated is essential to the command-and-control structure of the Department.

Finally, I just want to indicate that in the GAO findings, we concur with those findings. As the chief acquisition officer, this week I issued an acquisition decision memorandum which codifies that the portions of the project that are under our purview, as I indicated in 2014, that is $35 million, and the request in 2015 is $57 million, will be subject to the Acquisition Review Board process. We can't take Mr. Dong's acquisitions and apply them to our process, but we will do it for the portions that we oversee.

Finally, let me just say that my experience has been there is no finer project management team than Chris Mills at DHS and Shapour Ebadi at the GSA. These are individuals that know how to deliver projects. They have done it with Phase I at the Coast Guard. They will continue to do it with support from the Congress. I am just pleased to be here to say, yeah, we have got programs across the DHS portfolio that are troubled. I do not view this as one of them. I stand ready to answer questions for the Members. Thank you.

[The prepared statement of Mr. Cummiskey follows:]

PREPARED STATEMENT OF CHRIS CUMMISKEY

SEPTEMBER 19, 2014

Chairman Duncan, Ranking Member Barber, and Members of the committee, good morning. Thank you for the opportunity to discuss the DHS Consolidated Headquarters at St. Elizabeths. I am Chris Cummiskey, acting under secretary for management for the Department of Homeland Security. My responsibilities include the management of the Department's facilities and property. I am pleased to appear before this committee with my colleagues from the General Services Administration and Government Accountability Office to discuss the development of St. Elizabeths and the DHS Headquarters Consolidation plan. Greater consolidation of DHS facilities provides tangible benefits to taxpayers and the Department.

In the DHS National Capital Region Housing Master Plan, submitted to the Congress in 2006 in cooperation with GSA, Secretary Chertoff stated that the program was necessary to secure and strengthen DHS operations by unifying our core headquarters with those of our components and to yield more effective management. Today, Secretary Johnson remains focused on robust cross-component Unity of Effort and a culture of savings to minimize waste, eliminate duplication, and focus scarce resources on mission execution. The Department continues to support consolidation of our headquarters facilities and St. Elizabeths is part of that program.

The Government Accountability Office (GAO) reported in a 2013 review of GSA High-Value Leases (Report 13–744), that as agencies work to shrink their footprints through implementation of flexible workplace strategies and increased efficiencies, there are opportunities to make targeted investments out of high-value commercial leases and into efficient Federal space that will result in lower long-term costs to the taxpayer. The Department agrees with this GAO assessment and notes that it forms the foundation of the DHS Headquarters Consolidation Plan. St. Elizabeths is Federal space and was retained by GSA specifically for agencies with high security requirements. It is an anchor property already, housing the U.S. Coast Guard's Headquarters.

To frame the discussion of DHS Headquarters consolidation efforts, it is important to understand the respective roles and responsibilities between tenant agencies, such as DHS and GSA. In GAO Report 13–744, GSA's lead role in housing civilian agencies is noted as follows:

. . . Within the vast portfolio of government owned and leased assets, GSA plays the role of broker and property manager to many civilian agencies of the U.S. government . . . [1]

As a tenant agency, the Department of Homeland Security's role is to establish programmatic requirements; to budget for and fund tenant responsible items; to maintain a close partnership and monitor GSA's use of DHS funds; to validate that GSA managed design and construction meets the operational and program requirements for DHS; and to coordinate with GSA and all stakeholders throughout the process. Property development activities are managed by GSA in accordance with GSA policies, under GSA supervision, and under applicable statutes. The Department fully cooperates with GSA but does not exercise acquisition oversight nor di-

---

[1] GAO 13–744; *Federal Real Property: Greater Transparency and Strategic Focus Needed for High-Value GSA Leases*; September 2013, page 4.

rect supervisory control over GSA housing or procurement decisions. DHS is an active participant in tenant improvement decisions.

The original DHS Headquarters Consolidation plan, as developed by GSA in coordination with DHS, OMB, and Congress, proposed to complete the full development of St. Elizabeths in 2016 based on the start of construction funding in 2009. This plan was developed in conjunction with a comprehensive 3.5-year Master Plan, environmental impact statement, and historic preservation review process. Following the Master Plan approval, GSA completed the U.S. Coast Guard Headquarters relocation to St. Elizabeths on-time and on-budget for the portions of the project funded by the Congress. This was a commendable achievement given that GSA was not fully funded for all planned building and infrastructure development to support the U.S. Coast Guard relocation.

Unfortunately the original plan has not been appropriated the requested funding necessary to carry it out. As a result, in 2013 GSA and DHS developed a revised construction baseline to reflect the funding reduction in fiscal year 2011 and fiscal year 2012 and reduced annual development segments to more fiscally manageable levels that extended construction out to 2026. The schedule extension increased the estimate of future construction, due to inflation-only adjustments (no change in requirements) to $4.5 billion. Although inflation increased the estimate for future work, consolidation into Federal space still provides the Department long-term financial benefits over leasing according to GSA's analysis.

With the revised construction baseline in place, GSA and DHS began updating the Headquarters Consolidation plan in the fall of 2013 to address the on-going changes in workplace design and flexible workplace strategies that have gained broad acceptance over the last several years. In fact, the Management Directorate's Office of the Chief Readiness Support Officer adopted these strategies within their own office by implementing a pilot program to reduce office space by 50 percent and save over $1 million in annual rent costs. DHS and GSA are applying the lessons learned from this pilot program to update the DHS Headquarters Consolidation plan. The revised plan will result in lower costs and a shortened time frame if funded by the Congress, while accommodating greater utilization and more employees assigned to the campus within the Master Plan seat limitations.

The Department has made a commitment through the Freeze the Footprint initiative to increase space utilization from the current figure of about 210 Useable Square Feet (USF) per person of office space, to 150 USF. These actions will reduce costs and improve space efficiency in the future and apply to the St. Elizabeths development.

An additional important note is that 69 percent of DHS Headquarters and component leases in the National Capital Region will expire between fiscal year 2016 and fiscal year 2020. DHS tenant costs will be incurred with these lease replacements, regardless of future decisions on St. Elizabeths funding. As the commercial leases expire, they must be re-competed. These are not discretionary investments. These are "must pay" requirements. Without headquarters consolidation efforts for the DHS and component headquarters portfolio, we will perpetuate the status quo of dispersed locations and a long-term increased lease costs over housing components in fewer locations and at Federal space on the St. Elizabeths campus.

DHS strives to capitalize Unity of Effort opportunities that allow us to remain focused on our core mission—to protect the homeland. We look forward to further engagement with this committee regarding the DHS Headquarters Consolidation program.

In closing, I would like to assure this committee that DHS is working hard to remain a good steward of the taxpayers' money by managing our real estate portfolio, both Government-owned and -leased, in a cost-effective manner. The men and women who work tirelessly to protect the homeland deserve and require adequate facilities to support and execute their mission.

Thank you very much. I would be pleased to answer any questions the committee may have.

Mr. DUNCAN. Thank you.
Commissioner Dong.

STATEMENT OF NORMAN DONG, COMMISSIONER, PUBLIC BUILDINGS SERVICE, U.S. GENERAL SERVICES ADMINISTRATION

Mr. DONG. Good morning, Chairman Duncan, Ranking Member Barber, and Members of the subcommittee. My name is Norman

Dong, and I am the commissioner of GSA's Public Buildings Service. Thank you for inviting me to discuss the on-going consolidation of DHS Headquarters at St. Elizabeths. I would like to make three points this morning.

First, St. Elizabeths is a critical element in GSA's effort to consolidate Government real estate and to reduce overhead costs. By consolidating DHS facilities across the National Capital Region we can reduce future real estate costs, enhance mission effectiveness, and redevelop an underutilized asset already in the Federal portfolio.

This project allows to us shift more than 50 DHS leases across the National Capital Region to a Federally-owned campus at St. Elizabeths. As GAO has noted, long-term leasing is often far more expensive than Government ownership, especially when it comes to unique requirements like what we see for DHS. In the case of St. Es, the 30-year present value cost of leasing would be nearly $700 million more expensive than construction. This translates into an annual savings of more than $35 million.

With this project we are also able to house more people in less space. When the entire project is complete, St. Es will provide 14,000 seats for DHS employees on any given day. By adopting flexible workplace strategies like telework and desk sharing, DHS can accommodate even more employees in these seats. GSA is working with DHS on an updated housing strategy to maximize space utilization at St. Elizabeths and to achieve even greater cost savings for the Department.

Second, as GAO has noted, funding uncertainty has created serious challenges for the St. Elizabeths project. Piecemeal funding has extended the project's schedule and added cost. Congress appropriated resources for the project at a level far below the President's request in fiscal year 2011 and fiscal year 2012. Without stable funding, we will see more delays and more cost increases.

When the project began in 2006 we anticipated completion in 2016 at a total cost to the Government of $3.4 billion. Without funding, however, GSA and DHS had to revise the project strategy to reflect smaller, more affordable segments over a longer period of time. This had the effect of pushing the time line for completion out to 2026. With an extended schedule the project cost is now estimated at $4.5 billion. These costs increase due to inflation for construction costs as well as the cost of demobilization and remobilization of equipment and labor. Accelerating the remaining project schedule could reduce these additional costs.

Third, GSA and DHS have developed a strong record of success in project delivery at St. Elizabeths. We delivered Phase I of the DHS Headquarters project on time and on budget. Ultimately the success of this project will be judged by our actual results. We delivered Phase I, a new headquarters building for the Coast Guard, on time and on budget. In August 2013 the Coast Guard moved into a headquarters building that can accommodate 3,700 personnel. We eliminated five leases and moved nearly 1 million square feet of leased space to Federal ownership. The successful implementation of the Coast Guard Headquarters is an important step towards having a unified, consolidated, and secure headquarters for the Department.

We are now beginning work on the next phase. Congress provided $155 million in fiscal year 2014 for adaptive reuse of the historic Center Building, and I am pleased to announce that we will be awarding the contract for this work by the end of September. Our budget request for fiscal year 2015 includes $250 million to complete infrastructure and renovation necessary to fully occupy the Center Building complex.

Looking beyond our budget request, GSA is identifying other potential sources of funding to support this project. For example, with our Federal Triangle South project we are looking to exchange our Regional Office Building, as well as the vacant Cotton Annex, for additional construction services at St. Es. While we are pleased with our project execution, there are also opportunities to improve project delivery. We are working with DHS to enhance the master plan for St. Es, which will further improve space utilization and create even greater savings.

As we have seen from past experience, when Congress provides resources for a construction project GSA has a strong record of delivering these projects on-time and on-budget. Our work with our Coast Guard Headquarters is a perfect example and we plan to build on this initial momentum. The funding Congress has provided in fiscal year 2014, along with our fiscal year 2015 budget request, will allow us to continue forward progress on this essential project.

Thank you for the opportunity to speak with you today, and I am happy to answer any questions that you may have.

[The prepared statement of Mr. Dong follows:]

PREPARED STATEMENT OF NORMAN DONG

SEPTEMBER 19, 2014

INTRODUCTION

Good morning Chairman Duncan, Ranking Member Barber, and Members of the subcommittee. My name is Norman Dong, and I am the commissioner of the U.S. General Services Administration's Public Buildings Service. Thank you for inviting me to discuss the on-going consolidation of the Department of Homeland Security's Headquarters components at St. Elizabeths in Washington, DC.

GSA's mission is to deliver the best value in real estate, acquisition, and technology services to Government and the American people. To meet this mission, GSA is working with agencies across the Federal Government to reduce space requirements, improve space utilization, reduce real estate costs, and deliver better space that allows our Federal partners to better achieve their missions.

I'd like to make three points today. First, the development of a consolidated DHS Headquarters at St. Elizabeths is a critical piece of GSA's broader effort to consolidate Government real estate and reduce overhead costs across Government. Second, GSA and DHS have developed a strong record of success in project delivery at St. Elizabeths. GSA and DHS delivered Phase I of the DHS Headquarters project on-time and on-budget. Third, as the Government Accountability Office correctly notes, funding uncertainty has created serious challenges for St. Elizabeths, increasing costs and forcing GSA and DHS to extend the project delivery schedule.

OPPORTUNITIES FOR SAVINGS WITH A CONSOLIDATED DHS HEADQUARTERS

As a part of the administration's Freeze the Footprint initiative, GSA is helping our partner Federal agencies minimize overhead costs and make more efficient use of the Government's real property assets. We are working with agencies to reduce space requirements and shrink real estate footprints, reducing building's operating costs through energy-efficient retrofits and "smart building" technology, and leveraging partnerships with the private sector to deliver better, more efficient space to meet agency mission needs.

The St. Elizabeths project represents an opportunity to help achieve these important goals. By consolidating DHS Headquarters, we can reduce future real estate costs, enhance mission effectiveness through co-location, and redevelop an underutilized asset already in the Federal portfolio.

Consolidating DHS Headquarters operations in one location will eliminate more than 50 DHS leases, shifting millions of square feet of leased space to a Federally-owned campus. As GAO has noted, long-term leasing is typically far more expensive than Government ownership, especially when it comes to unique Governmental requirements like those that are required at St. Elizabeths. In the case of St. Elizabeths, the 30-year present value cost of construction is $698 million less than leasing. This results in an annual savings of more than $35 million.

Additionally, we are generating additional savings by housing more people in less space. When the entire project is complete, St. Elizabeths will provide space for 14,000 seats. Through implementation of flexible workplace strategies, these 14,000 seats can be leveraged to accommodate many more employees, and GSA is currently working with DHS on this updated approach.

At the same time, co-location will facilitate an effective response in case of a National emergency, optimize internal coordination and communication, and foster a cohesive culture among the many agencies that now make up the Department.

ON-TIME, ON-BUDGET DELIVERY OF PHASE I OF ST. ELIZABETHS

Ultimately, the success of the St. Elizabeths project will be judged by its results. Project delivery at St. Elizabeths thus far has been a success.

GSA and DHS have successfully delivered Phase I of the project, construction of the new Douglas A. Munro Coast Guard Headquarters Building. This state-of-the-art facility will use sustainable technologies to drop energy use to more than 30 percent below industry standards and cut water usage by nearly 50 percent. Additionally, this phase included perimeter security, the renovation of several historic buildings, infrastructure improvements throughout the campus, and a 2,000-car parking garage. We completed Phase I on-time and on-budget, and in the process, eliminated five leases and moved nearly 1 million square feet of space to Federal ownership. As a result, the Coast Guard completed its move to a building on the St. Elizabeths campus that can accommodate 3,700 personnel in 2013.

We are now beginning work on the next phase of the DHS Consolidation. Congress provided $155 million in fiscal year 2014 for adaptive reuse of the historic Center Building. GSA's fiscal year 2015 budget request includes $250 million to complete needed infrastructure and renovate buildings adjoining the Center Building. This funding will allow DHS to fully occupy the Center Building Complex.

In addition to GSA's annual budget requests, we are seeking alternative mechanisms for project delivery. GSA is leveraging the value of other properties in our portfolio to expedite delivery of the St. Elizabeths campus. Specifically, as a part of our Federal Triangle South project, we are engaging the private sector to exchange GSA's Regional Office Building and the vacant Cotton Annex for construction services that may include renovations of historic buildings at the St. Elizabeths campus.

THE IMPACTS OF CUTS IN FUNDING ON PROJECT COSTS AND SCHEDULE

Of course, funding constraints have had a considerable impact on the St. Elizabeths project, much like the rest of the Federal real estate portfolio. As GAO has noted many times, uncertainty in funding and limited access to the Federal Buildings Fund create a serious challenge for the management of real property.[1]

For St. Elizabeths, piecemeal funding of project phases have resulted in an extended schedule and eliminated additional opportunities to reduce costs through sharing resources and infrastructure among phases. Congress appropriated resources for the project at a level far below the President's budget request in fiscal years 2011 and 2012. In the absence of stable funding, the schedule for project completion will face delays, and costs increase with delays.

You can see the effect of funding constraints on the Center Building. In fiscal year 2011, GSA's budget request included $381 million to continue the project, including for the renovation of the Center Building. Congress cut GSA's new construction budget request that year by 92 percent, and we were only able to allocate $30 million to St. Elizabeths. Since that time, the cost of completing the Center Building has increased by $17 million.

---

[1] See *Capital Financing: Alternative Approaches to Budgeting for Federal Real Property* (GAO–14–239) and *Federal Buildings Fund: Improved Transparency and Long-term Plan Needed to Clarify Capital Funding Priorities* (GAO–12–646).

When we began the St. Elizabeths project in 2006, the project was scheduled for completion in 2016 at a total Government cost of $3.4 billion. Due to funding cuts, GSA and DHS had to revise the project strategy resulting in smaller segments over a longer period that are more manageable in this environment. This has pushed the project time line for completion out to 2026, and, largely due to inflation over that period of time, the total estimated project cost is now $4.5 billion. Accelerating the remaining project schedule could reduce these additional costs.

GSA appreciates GAO's recommendations that Congress consider alternative budget structures that allow for greater consistency in funding and project planning. Until GSA has full and consistent access to the Federal Buildings Fund, we will continue to see cost increases and schedule delays for long-term, multi-phase Government construction projects. St. Elizabeths is no exception.

INCORPORATING GAO RECOMMENDATIONS INTO ON-GOING PROJECT PLANNING AND EXECUTION

While we are very pleased with our execution of the St. Elizabeths project thus far, GSA recognizes and appreciates that there are always opportunities to improve project delivery. GAO has recommended that we conduct a comprehensive needs assessment and alternatives analysis to identify the costs and benefits of construction and leasing project delivery methods. We have already begun this assessment, and will develop an alternatives analysis that further improves efficiency and savings. We are working with DHS to improve processes and reduce costs by decreasing the footprint, reexamining certain requirements, and integrating the efficient use of leased space based on a review of DHS leases throughout the National Capital Region.

We will update cost and schedule estimates as we continue this work, and appreciate the chance to potentially incorporate practices recommended by GAO. Not all of GAO's cited procedures and reviews apply in the context of real estate construction. Some recommended practices are better suited to weapons systems, spacecraft, aircraft carriers, and software systems. However, we agree with GAO that quantifying risk and uncertainty are important considerations in this funding environment, and we will incorporate these considerations moving forward. We are working closely with DHS, and together, we are happy to update this committee as we finalize this plan.

CONCLUSION

Thank you for the opportunity to speak with you today about our on-going work to consolidate DHS Headquarters components at St. Elizabeths. I welcome the opportunity to discuss GSA's commitment to shrinking the Federal Government's real property footprint and consolidating out of costly leases. I am happy to answer any questions you may have.

Mr. DUNCAN. Thank you, Commissioner Dong.

I will now recognize myself for 5 minutes for questioning.

I think as a Nation we can be penny-wise and pound-foolish. I think this is a project that exemplifies that in a lot of ways. I heard the term "on-time and on-budget" numerous times from two witnesses in regard to the Coast Guard facility. Well, on-time and on-budget is really a misstatement because you don't have an access road that was originally planned. You had reduced transportation infrastructure within the facility. You changed the excavation plan there on the hillside, which is ultimately going to cost more taxpayer dollars down the road. Originally it was planned to excavate the complete hillside for future components. You decided only to do part of that. So, sure, you can reduce the budget going forward to be on-time and on-budget. So I just think that is misleading the American taxpayer.

I think it is very clear that we are not seeing leading capital decision-making practices happen. I think Congress has a strong responsibility to the taxpayers to make sure that their money is spent appropriately at a time when we are almost $18 trillion in debt, and you look back at when this project was originally put on the drawing board and originally funded in the stimulus package we weren't $18 trillion in debt. We need to prioritize where we spend our taxpayer dollars.

Several years ago, then-Secretary Janet Napolitano said that she would rather have money to complete building a National security cutter for the Coast Guard, support the Secret Service in its activities, and sustain our efforts at the border than have a new building. Given the threat posed by ISIS, the illegal alien crisis in our Southern Border, specifically the Rio Grande Valley, but really all across the Southern Border, the cyber attacks that we heard over and over this week in the committee hearing, both from the FBI and from Secretary Johnson, cyber attacks by the Chinese and others, other threats, isn't the world more dangerous than when this statement was made? I would say that it is based on the emerging threats.

We also heard this week from Secretary Johnson that he has the ability, he has a board room, he has a board table, and he can bring the leadership team together to communicate and that he does regularly. We have a morale issue in the Department of Homeland Security, turf wars and components that were originally stand-alone components now that are part of the broader DHS.

My dad ran a textile mill his whole career. He would walk the plant floor every morning talking with the folks that were opening the cotton bales, the card room that were breaking up those fibers, and the spinning room, and the weaving room, and the napping operation, and the finishing operation, not talking to his supervisor, talking to the individuals that were running the machinery of the organization to find out what was really happening on the ground.

I think it is important that the supervisors within those various components actually spend time within their agencies. If we have this facility—and this is just me being rhetorical, I guess—but if you moved the leadership team away from the normal operations, are you not going to see even less of a positive morale in the components?

So I think Americans would love to see us redirect some of these resources to more border security, more fencing, more electronic components. I am very concerned that we have an aging Coast Guard cutter fleet and we need new ships. I could expand that to the Department of Defense and the reduction of surface ships, the need to replenish the fuel in a reactor in an aircraft carrier.

I say all that in the context that we are $18 trillion in debt and one day the lender is going to come calling. We continue to have deficit spending in this country. At what point in time do we drop back and punt? At what point in time do we make a real resolve to pass an acquisition reform bill that puts the right accountability practices in place?

Secretary Johnson has been someone that is in favor of acquisition reform. He wants to do it in-house. I appreciate his position, he is the Secretary. But I am also accountable to the taxpayers of the United States of America, and I think an acquisition reform bill that gives Congress more oversight and puts some parameters in place for you guys that are spending those tax dollars is very important.

So taking what I said earlier from Secretary Napolitano, GAO reported that DHS officials said it would be illogical to develop anything beyond a generalized milestone schedule. Generalized milestone schedule, that is what leads to cost overruns and delays.

The Secretary this week said in the committee hearing that they look at the number of OTMs that come across the border. They don't have a good idea of that total number. They look at it in a broad sense. I don't care whether you look at it in a broad sense or a narrow sense, Americans realize that we don't know who is in our country.

I think if you look at a generalized milestone schedule then Americans realize you don't know how much money you are spending and you don't know when this project is going to be completed. I think that, I go back to an opening statement, if you were going to build a house, you are going to sit down with the contractor, you are going to have a good idea of what those costs are. There are going to be some unexpected costs, we may run into some rock digging the foundation, you may change and want different kind of shingles. But you are going to have that understanding and you are going to know it is going to take X number of months to build that house. You are going to have a good understanding.

I don't believe the American taxpayer has a good understanding about the St. Elizabeths project. As much as we may want it in the District of Columbia, as much as we may think we might need it as a Nation, I think we have an obligation to the American taxpayer to tell them how their money is going to be spent. I think we also have an obligation to the American taxpayer to sometimes drop back and reevaluate. I think that is what we are trying to do: Drop back, reevaluate priorities, look at where we have spent money wisely and unwisely.

When you look at the hardest wood in America when you could have brought a different component for the decking. When you have rain-wash flush toilets, that is a political agenda driving the spending of taxpayer dollars. We could have saved money using normal—normal—plumbing.

Mr. Cummiskey, is that your position, that we should continue to operate under a generalized milestone schedule?

Mr. CUMMISKEY. Mr. Chairman, thank you. You make a lot of salient points and I think it makes sense.

I would answer it this way. Your analogy of constructing a house I think makes a lot of sense as well. But if I am building a house, and I build the frame, and then I wait 4 years to complete the facility, there is going to be a change in the cost and in the time frame associated with that. That is what happening with St. Elizabeths. The Congress, through appropriate funds as well as ARRA funding, funded the first phase. The GSA has built the infrastructure on the campus to support Phases II and III. So you are going to have changes in that over time.

To answer your question directly, I think that we have gone through the industry-accepted practices, and I think I would defer to GSA on this, in terms of planning a facility, and that is what you are seeing with the Coast Guard facility. That came in, in a position of the planning assessment that is consistent with what the industry and the standards accept.

So I would certainly defer to GSA, but I think that in terms of Phases II and III we have changed away from that because we have had to move to usable segments. We are not looking at Phase II the way it was in the master plan. We are saying, okay, the footprint is in place now, we are going to change the requirements in terms of square footage from 210 square feet down to 150, we are making the adjustments over time that GAO has required us to do, and I think that that planning envelope makes a lot of sense.

Mr. DUNCAN. Okay. Let me ask you this. Two-thousand-eight saw a financial downturn in this country. This project was kicked off with stimulus funds, one-time dollars, with a continual funding stream. I keep hearing about the lack of funding from Congress. But we were operating from 2009 to today with the understanding that we are still in an economic downturn, that budgets are crimped all across Government spending.

Do you ever walk out on the Mall behind the Capitol? Have you ever spent time walking out on the Mall? Washington is a great city, right? I do it. Have you found that tree, that money tree, because I hadn't found it yet. It is not out there. The money that we are talking about is coming from the American taxpayers and they expect us to be a little more frugal and wise with the dollars we are spending.

So operating in that environment, understanding that from 2008 to today we are still in an economic downturn, the great recession that hadn't really improved dramatically, we have got to make smart decisions. So Congress didn't fund this. Congress doesn't have the money to fund it. The tree isn't out in the backyard.

We are trying to make smart decisions with the money allocated to us. I came to Congress to reduce Government spending to try to reduce the deficit and live within our means because that is what moms and dads and businesses have to do all across this great land. Government shouldn't continue to operate in deficit spending and run up debt. That is not fair to the American taxpayers. It is not fair to my little boys, 19, 16, and 13, that are going to be future taxpayers of this country. Just because we are in the Government doesn't mean we continue to spend money like it grows on that tree in the backyard.

I am going to have some additional questions. We are going to be here for a little while. We don't have a whole lot of Member participation, so I look forward to a second round of questioning. But I am over time, so I am going to yield to the Ranking Member and then come back. Thanks.

Mr. BARBER. Well, thank you, Mr. Chairman.

One of the things that the Chairman and I tried to do and hopefully will happen with the passage of the Acquisition Accountability and Efficiency Act for DHS was to make sure that the money that we give on behalf of the people we represent, the taxpayers of this country, is spent wisely, with full accountability. It also means that in the end the Department will spend its money prudently and on the right priorities. Let me tell you what one of my biggest priorities is and has yet to be resolved.

Representing, as I do, one of nine border districts, I am very concerned that we have yet to deal with the border security issue that plagues the people I represent every single day. If you know, as you do, Mr. Cummiskey, you know Arizona well, east of Douglas all the way to the State line with New Mexico is wide-open territory. The drug cartels basically own that territory. In the Tucson Sector, which includes my district and the adjoining district, we account for 47 percent—47 percent—of the drugs seized along the Southwest Border, and that has been going on for many years. We have to stop this flow of drugs carried by people who are prone to violence, heavily armed.

The people I represent want to know from me when I go home, what is the Department doing to deploy its resources to address that problem? While I know these are different pockets of money, it is a really tough question to answer when they say to me, how is it possible that the consolidation of a headquarters for DHS has cost so much more than was originally intended or projected? How is it possible that we are going to be 11 or 12 years late? Tough question. I don't have a good answer for them because from where they see it, it is all one department's money. They want answers and they deserve them.

I also am concerned about how it is we treat in every way possible, by pay and in terms of morale, the men and women who are on the border, at the border trying to secure the homeland, the Border Patrol Agents, those who are manning the ports of entry. The ports of entry need more staff. We are opening a new port, expanded port in Nogales, Mariposa, don't have enough staff for that.

Last year we avoided—very narrowly avoided—furloughing hundreds of Border Patrol Agents. Currently Border Patrol Agents are wondering, what is the certainty of their pay going forward? These issues create problems for our security and create problems for the men and women that we have asked to protect the homeland. Yes, we understand because we delve into it here that these are separate sections of an appropriation process.

But I have to say, it is really hard for people back home to understand how it is possible that the Department spends thousands of dollars it shouldn't in Ajo for homes, wastes $24 million on an IT program that doesn't work, and now is over-budget in consolidation.

So I hope that through the study that has been given and the recommendations that have been made we can correct, take this ship, the course of this ship, and bring it back under control.

I want to ask Mr. Maurer a question or two about the GAO study. Given the size and complexity of the Department's headquarters consolidation, how long will it take, do you believe, for DHS and GSA to implement the best practices, including cost and schedule estimates, and an evaluation of alternatives contained in the GAO's report? The second part of that question is: Once the Department has implemented these practices how long would it take, do you believe, for the Department—or should it take for the Department—to complete the St. Elizabeths consolidation project?

Mr. MAURER. Thank you for the question. I think that DHS and GSA are well-positioned to take action on our recommendations and implement them in relatively short order. They have established plans, although they are outdated. They have an established track record in doing work at St. Elizabeths. They have processes in place that should allow them to implement our recommendations. We are not asking them to do an awful lot more than they have already done, but they do have to up their game to better manage the overall project and the implementation of the St. Elizabeths effort.

In terms of how long it would take to complete the project after implementing our recommendations, that is really a function of how much money Congress provides and when those funds are provided. That, in turn, is going to depend, I think in large part, on how responsive DHS and GSA are in responding to our recommendations, implementing leading practices, and updating our plans.

Mr. BARBER. Let me continue, Mr. Maurer, with you on a different aspect of this issue. The GAO report discusses the Federal Government's evolution regarding workplace standards and it states that the Department's, DHS's, demand for office space would or could decrease by almost 800,000 square feet, or from 4.5 million to 3.7 million if the new standards were adopted. Does the GAO report account for DHS' secure space requirements?

Mr. MAURER. Yeah, our assessment was looking at the original plan, which called for 4.5 million square feet within the St. Elizabeths campus. That includes the amount of spaces necessary for secure work stations and work processes. So our analysis would also include that as well.

Mr. BARBER. Well, let me ask Mr. Cummiskey next, but before I do, I just want to say it is great to have a fellow Arizonian in the House. Your reputation in our State was exemplary as a State legislator, as the chief information officer for the Governor, and your work was recognized by the National Governors Association for its creatively and innovation. I am really happy to have you here today and in this position at DHS. Your abilities and skills are well-proven and I think you will apply that talent to this very important undertaking.

My question, Mr. Cummiskey, or Secretary is, GAO has stated that Congress should consider withholding funds for the St. Elizabeths project until the Department and GSA develop a revised headquarters consolidation plan that conforms with GAO leading practices.

Could you just expand? You said you have agreed with the recommendation. Could you expand on what the Department will do to implement that recommendation?

Mr. CUMMISKEY. Sure. Certainly. Mr. Chairman, Ranking Member Barber, thank you for the kind words. It is great to be here.

One of the things we have tried to do, we work closely with GAO on a regular basis, and so they have telegraphed and we have entered into both interviews with all of the personnel associated with the project, as well as with GAO, as they went through the process of making the recommendations. So we saw this coming for some months, and so we have worked closely with GAO to make sure that our planning processes are aligned with what we thought the recommendations might be.

So what you will see in concert with the fiscal year 2016 submission after the first of the year is an updated or enhanced project plan which takes into account what Mr. Maurer has been describing, what GSA has been doing internally to up its game, as has been indicated, to take account of Freeze the Footprint and other changes in the environment that have led us to look at this long-term project in a way that is more conducive to what the Chairman has indicated, smart, efficient, and delivering for the taxpayer. So we anticipate that it won't be much of a lift to comply with what Mr. Maurer is indicating.

Mr. BARBER. Thank you for that. Let me ask you a second question. If it should turn out that the Department's plan for consolidation at St. Elizabeths is abandoned, what is the Department's alternative plan, and how much would that cost compared with consolidation at St. Elizabeths?

Mr. CUMMISKEY. Thank you, Congressman. Essentially what we found in the assessment from GSA, as well as our chief financial officer, is that in the resourcing decisions that the Chairman was alluding to, we would love to be in a position to redirect additional funds to National security cutters, ICE detention beds, all sorts of other prioritizations for both Secretary Johnson and the administration. The difficulty we have with the top line is that that is not moving.

So what happens is that in the analysis that we have done we are going to end up spending about the same amount of money over the same horizon for lease consolidation, additional tenant improvements as we would spend as a Department on St. Elizabeths in the relocation and consolidation.

So I would like to say today that we had money that we could redirect to other priorities. Certainly, Secretaries Napolitano and Johnson both were under that pressure to deliver. But the reality is, even with the consolidation plans that we would pivot to, it is unlikely that we would spend any less than what we were spending with the proposed plan.

Mr. BARBER. Thank you.

Mr. Chairman, if I might, just one last question—or two actually—for Mr. Dong, Commissioner Dong.

When will the updated plan for the Department's headquarters consolidation be released by GSA and DHS? Second, as the DHS consolidation project is delayed, if it was delayed, or has it been delayed already, what is the estimated cost to GSA of having to renegotiate current leases?

Mr. DONG. As we work with DHS on the enhanced master plan for St. Elizabeths, our expectation is that we will be submitting that to the Congress at the same time that we submit the fiscal year 2016 budget request.

In terms of the cost of short-term extensions that would result from the project being delayed, we are currently working with DHS right now to quantify that impact, and we will be happy to share the results with this committee.

Mr. BARBER. I actually do have one other question for you, Mr. Dong, and that is, what would GSA's obligations be at St. Elizabeths if the project were halted? Would, for example, the Coast Guard continue to operate there? Could other Federal entities move into that space? What would happen, in other words, if we said, no more money, let's stay with the current plan of leasing buildings across the capital?

Mr. DONG. We estimate that the on-going costs associated with DHS, if there were no additional consolidation at St. Elizabeths, would be about $132 million each year.

Mr. BARBER. Thank you, Mr. Chairman.

Mr. DUNCAN. I thank the gentleman.

The Chairman will now recognize a guest to the committee, Ms. Norton, for 5 minutes.

Ms. NORTON. Thank you very much, and I appreciate your courtesy, Mr. Chairman.

Mr. Maurer, I note as you began your report, and I am quoting here, you say, "With a current projected completion date of 2026, the St. Elizabeths project is intended to provide DHS a secure facility to allow for more efficient incident management response and command-and-control operations and also provide long-term savings by reducing reliance on leased space."

As a predicate to this question for you, Mr. Maurer, let me ask Mr. Cummiskey or Mr. Dong, during the construction of the Coast Guard, the U.S. Coast Guard, were there any change requirements that resulted in greater costs over the annual inflation adjustments while you were putting that building up, or did it go up as expected without any such additional funds requested?

Mr. DONG. Once the project was funded we were able to deliver on time and on budget. There were no change requests or changes that drove the cost higher.

Ms. NORTON. Yeah, well, that is an indication of a certain amount of efficiency on the part of GAO and DHS when it had the money. The money was provided, or a great deal of the money was provided for the Department, for the U.S. Coast Guard.

I want to ask Mr. Maurer, whether using the U.S. Coast Guard as a marker, that is the building that is up, that was delivered on time from the outset of construction once the money was available to the agencies. Isn't that some indication that had the agencies had the funds for the rest of the construction they would have been at least as efficient as they were with respect to the Coast Guard building that went up on-time and on-budget? If you can use any marker, isn't that the marker you have to use?

Mr. MAURER. That is certainly an indication of what they have been able to do in the past. Certainly they also had to descope some of the work that was originally planned under Phase I to match the amount of funds that they received from the Congress.

But going forward, we remain concerned about their current position or their current lack of compliance with leading practices for cost estimation and schedule estimation. That creates additional risk that future build-out at St. Elizabeths will be at increased risk of going longer than planned and costing more than planned. So that is why we really think it is important for them to implement our recommendations on leading practices, for GSA and DHS to follow their own policies and guidelines, and to update their plans accordingly.

Ms. NORTON. Thank you.

Now, how many times, Mr. Cummiskey or Mr. Dong or both of you, has the agency received its full budget request at the beginning of the fiscal year the way you had it for the U.S. Coast Guard? How many times have you received your full budget request?

Mr. DONG. There is a significant gap between what GSA had requested in the President's budget request versus what was actually——

Ms. NORTON. I didn't ask you that. I didn't ask you about the gap. I asked you how many times have either of you received your budget request at the beginning of the fiscal year?

Mr. DONG. I don't think ever.

Ms. NORTON. How has that affected capital planning for that project?

Mr. DONG. Without having funding certainty, it is very difficult to scope out the entire project and to get into the details that would allow you to have a specific schedule. Once we do get funding we are able to do a very detailed project schedule, just as GAO has pointed out.

Ms. NORTON. So you have had to engage in short-term leases. Would you explain what the disadvantage of short-term leases are when you have to have short-term leases? How many short-term leases do you have? How many leases do you expect to come up and have to be renewed across the region?

Mr. DONG. We have far too many short-term extensions on the leases for DHS components because of the delay in this project, because funding has not materialized. What we see is——

Ms. NORTON. How many leases are going to become due, let us say, next year that you will have to then either renew or do short-term leases?

Mr. DONG. We can provide you with the specifics there.

Ms. NORTON. I think that is very important to do. Since, of course, you have this delay, when a lease becomes due, do you have to do a long-term lease? Do you do a short-term lease? How much more expensive is a short-term lease than a long-term lease?

Mr. DONG. If we know that the agency is not going to be in that space for an extended period of time because of a plan to move elsewhere, we will do a short-term extension. But what we have seen and what we discussed with the T&I Committee several months ago, when we focused on leasing, is that any time you are in hold-over or extension, you are paying, on average, about 20 percent more than you should.

Ms. NORTON. Could you clarify this? Is it not the case that the basic infrastructure for the entire consolidation is in place and in the ground? What would happen to it if we simply abandoned the project?

Mr. DONG. We have a lot of the infrastructure in place. As I mentioned before, the carrying cost of that is about $132 million each year. The fiscal year 2015 budget request actually goes further in terms of completing the infrastructure work in terms of the Malcolm X Boulevard and the 295 access road. So those are important investments that we need to make to ensure the full viability of the St. Elizabeths program.

Ms. NORTON. I realize I am over time. If I could note for the record, Mr. Chairman, that the original cost was to be $4.5 billion, but the leases, so far as we can tell, for the space now will cost $5.2 billion over 30 years. So finishing the project would virtually pay for itself, rather than allowing these expensive leases to go forward.

Thank you very much, Mr. Chairman.

Mr. DUNCAN. Thank the gentlelady.

We have got time for a few more questions for another round. I was on a rant earlier because, I am not mad about this project, I am not upset, I am sad when I see taxpayer dollars spent in a way that I may not agree with.

So, anyway, let me just ask a couple of questions. The GAO reports shows the DHS failed to conduct proper oversight over St. Elizabeths project. That is the fact. Specifically, DHS never consistently identified St. Es as a major acquisition program, even though DHS alone plans to spend almost $2 billion in taxpayer funds on the headquarters. So $2 billion dollars, but it is not a major acquisition program.

Mr. Cummiskey, can you explain your rationale to Members of this committee why DHS failed to take the simple step of identifying St. Es as a major acquisition program?

Mr. CUMMISKEY. Certainly, Mr. Chairman. Thank you.

The reason that that was the case, as I indicated in the opening statement, that the bulk of the funding goes to GSA. Using 2014 and 2015 as examples, our request in fiscal year 2014 is $35 million. So comparatively it is a smaller amount than what we would normally see in acquisition oversight. That is not to say that we haven't been overseeing our portion of it. But in the same fiscal year, in 2014, the $155 million that went to GSA for the construction of the next piece of this isn't in our purview. So we are overseeing the portion that we have and making sure that there is accountability.

As I indicated, I have issued an acquisition decision memorandum this week that, based on the GAO recommendation, going forward we will subject it to the same rigor as the Acquisition Review Board process does for any major acquisition, even though the dollar figures tend to be smaller comparatively to what we usually would consider.

Mr. DUNCAN. Okay. Thank you.

We toured the facility last year, Members of the committee did. I looked at it from the eyes of a developer, as I have renovated and developed property in my private-sector life. So, Mr. Dong, I understand some of the challenges of taking an existing building and developing it for a 21st Century business practice or use. Could you explain the enormity of the challenge with this historic preservation and why did DHS and GSA proceed knowing the huge challenge that lay ahead of them instead of picking a more manageable site?

Mr. DONG. When we were considering the question of site selection we considered a number of factors that focused on the ability to support DHS, its mission, and its operational requirements. We looked at having a site that was large enough to support the magnitude of employees that would be consolidated from across the National Capital Region into that site. We looked at a site that would be able to accommodate level 5 security. We also wanted a site that had proximity to the White House and to the Congress. We also wanted a site that had access to transportation and major roadways.

Mr. DUNCAN. Proximity to the White House, is that what I heard you say?

Mr. DONG. Being able to be close to Washington, to the center Washington.

Mr. DUNCAN. Wow. If you needed to get to the White House rapidly, even driving with security and lights flashing and all that from that site to the White House it is going to take you a while. Probably going to get in a helicopter a lot quicker to get to the White House.

So having that dynamic in play, site selection, looking at a vacant tract of land in Virginia and starting from scratch probably would have made just as much sense, because you are still going to have to get in a helicopter and fly to the White House for a rapid face-to-face.

Wow. Okay. So I am thinking about the next question. I am going to just stop right there.

Mr. Barber, do you have any further questions?

Mr. BARBER. No.

Mr. DUNCAN. I would like to ask unanimous consent to submit to the record the Majority staff committee report from January 2014 on the rising cost and delays in construction of new DHS Headquarters at St. Elizabeths.

No objection, so ordered.*

I want to thank the panelists for being here. I want to thank the committee. This is an issue that is going to be here. We have put some slides up, I think, of what the site looked like. I think we have delved into the GAO report. I am going to ask the committee to read the report. I want to commend the GAO for its efforts in putting that together. I thank the staff for delving through this and really staying on top of this.

I want to urge the Department, Mr. Cummiskey, to continue with acquisition reform management. Hopefully, we can get the Senate to pass a bill that will give us some more tools, tools for you and tools for us. We want to work in concert with you to make sure we are effective on spending taxpayer dollars, make sure that we have the appropriate oversight, and to make sure that we are accountable.

Mr. Schneider had a letter, former Bush administrator or appointee. But, you know what, he is not accountable to the taxpayers. It is easy to sit on the sideline and say, you can do this or you could do that better or this is why this necessary. But when you were accountable to the taxpayer and the voters, then it is a little different on this side of the fence. I think we are doing the appropriate oversight and I think that is what this committee was designed to do. I want to thank the committee for their efforts.

I really do hate that we ended our work in the House yesterday and that many Members left, because I think we had a lot of Members that were interested in this hearing, but they also have some things to do back home. Mr. Hudson from North Carolina would have been here this morning, but he is at the doctor not feeling well. So we wish him a speedy recovery.

*The information has been retained in committee files and is available at *http://homeland.house.gov/press-release/duncan-releases-majority-staff-report-efficiency-construction-dhs-s-new-headquarters*.

Thank you, gentlemen. Committee Members may have some additional questions for you, and those will be submitted. We ask that you will provide the answers to us and respond to those in writing.

So without objection, the subcommittee will stand adjourned.

[Whereupon, at 10:43 a.m., the subcommittee was adjourned.]

APPENDIX

QUESTIONS FROM CHAIRMAN JEFF DUNCAN FOR DAVID C. MAURER

Question 1a. The GAO report notes that the St. Elizabeths cost estimate was overly optimistic and the schedule is unreliable.

Do you think it's appropriate for Congress to appropriate funds for St. Elizabeths without credible and reliable information on how many taxpayer dollars will be ultimately spent on the project?

Answer. High-quality, reliable cost and schedule estimates are critical to the success of a major program such as the consolidation project at St. Elizabeths. Such estimates provide the basis for informed investment decision making, realistic budget formulation and program resourcing, meaningful progress measurement, proactive course correction when warranted, accountability for results, and for the expenditure of taxpayer dollars. We recommended in September 2014 that Congress consider making future funding for the St. Elizabeths project contingent upon the Department of Homeland Security (DHS) and General Services Administration (GSA) developing a revised headquarters consolidation plan that includes the development and submission of reliable cost and schedule estimates, among other things.[1] We found that DHS and GSA cost and schedule estimates for the headquarters consolidation project at St. Elizabeths do not or only minimally or partially conform with leading estimating practices, and are therefore unreliable.[2] For example, we found that the 2013 cost estimate—the most recent available—was not regularly updated to reflect significant changes to the program including actual costs and did not include an independent estimate. In addition, we found that the 2008 and 2013 schedule estimates did not include all activities for both the Government and its contractors necessary to accomplish the project's objectives.[3]

Question 1b. Did DHS and GSA simply lack the expertise to accurately assess the costs and schedule or was the plan to downplay the cost and schedule risks of St. Elizabeths to ensure the project moved forward?

Answer. We believe that DHS and GSA officials have the capability to implement our September 2014 recommendation to develop more reliable cost and schedule estimates for the remaining portions of the St. Elizabeths project that conform to GSA guidance and leading practices.[4] DHS and GSA concurred with this recommendation, which also stated that the estimates should be revised before moving forward with additional funding requests for the DHS Headquarters consolidation project. Until DHS and GSA develop reliable cost and schedule estimates, the project is at greater risk of potential cost overruns, missed deadlines, and performance shortfalls.

Question 2a. DHS clearly disagreed with GAO's criteria for leading practices in capital planning and cost and schedule estimating used to evaluate the management of St. Elizabeths.

Please explain why these leading practices are applicable to DHS and GSA.

Answer. The $4.5 billion construction project at St. Elizabeths, in conjunction with the larger effort to consolidate DHS Headquarters personnel in the Washington, DC

---

[1] GAO, *Federal Real Property: DHS and GSA Need to Strengthen the Management of DHS Headquarters Consolidation,* GAO–14–648 (Washington, DC: Sept. 19, 2014).

[2] See leading practices at: GAO, *GAO Cost Estimating and Assessment Guide: Best Practices for Developing and Managing Capital Program Costs,* GAO–09–3SP (Washington, DC: Mar. 2, 2009) and *GAO Schedule Assessment Guide: Best Practices for Project Schedules,* GAO–12–120G (Washington, DC: May 2012). The methodology outlined in these guides is a compilation of best practices that Federal estimating organizations and industry use to develop and maintain reliable cost and schedule estimates throughout the life of a Government acquisition program. The leading practices were developed in conjunction with Government and industry experts in the estimating community. By default, these guides also serve as guiding principles for our auditors to evaluate the economy, efficiency, and effectiveness of Government programs.

[3] GAO–14–648.

[4] GAO–14–648.

area, is a major capital project that requires sound capital planning and reliable cost and schedule estimating by DHS and GSA. Congress, the Office of Management and Budget (OMB), and GAO have all identified the need for effective capital decision making among Federal agencies. GAO developed its *Executive Guide: Leading Practices in Capital Decision-Making* to provide detailed guidance to Federal agencies on leading practices for the four phases of capital programming—planning, budgeting, acquiring, and managing capital assets—assets such as the development of the St. Elizabeths campus. These practices are, in part, intended to provide a disciplined approach or process to help Federal agencies effectively plan and procure assets to achieve the maximum return on investment.[5]

In addition, we have applied our leading cost and schedule estimation practices in past work involving Federal construction projects similar to the St. Elizabeths project at other Federal agencies.[6] The leading practices were developed in conjunction with numerous stakeholders from Government and the private sector, including DHS and GSA. Furthermore, GSA acknowledged the value of our leading cost estimation practices in 2007 and issued an order to apply the principles to all cost estimates prepared in every GSA project, process, or organization.[7] DHS has also applied the leading practices as guidelines for assessing its own programs.[8] We concluded that developing cost and schedule estimates consistent with leading practices could promote greater transparency and provide decision makers needed information about the St. Elizabeths project and the larger DHS Headquarters consolidation effort.[9]

Question 2b. Why does DHS and GSA think that Government-wide leading practices should not apply to St. Elizabeths?

Answer. DHS and GSA agreed with our September 2014 recommendations on the importance of conforming with Government-wide leading practices throughout future phases of the St. Elizabeths project.[10] However, in its formal comments on the report DHS expressed concern that the report was overly focused on "leading practices" as opposed to being more outcome- and results-oriented. We believe that applying the Government-wide leading practices on capital decision making and cost/schedule estimation cited in our report would better position DHS and GSA to manage the St. Elizabeths project and help ensure better outcomes and results. DHS also stated that GSA, in concert with DHS, has already conducted sufficient analysis to support the leading practices in our report. We disagree, and as we noted in the report, cost, and schedule estimates for the project were deficient in several areas, including comprehensiveness, accuracy, and credibility.

In its formal comments on the draft report, GSA stated that several of the leading practices we identified are better-suited to non-real estate investments such as weapons systems, spacecraft, aircraft carriers, and software systems. We disagree with this as well. As stated in our report and noted above, we have applied our leading cost and schedule estimation practices in past work involving Federal construction projects, and the leading practices were developed in conjunction with numerous stakeholders from Government and the private sector including DHS and

---

[5] GAO, *Executive Guide: Leading Practices in Capital Decision-Making*, GAO/AIMD–99–32 (Washington, DC: December 1998). To produce this guide, we conducted extensive research to identify leading practices in capital decision making used by State and local governments and private-sector organizations. Specifically, based on interviews and documentation obtained from site visits to leading organizations, we identified innovative practices used by individual organizations as well as approaches and elements that were common across organizations. The leading organizations in our study reviewed a draft of this guide and verified that the case study examples are an accurate representation of their practices.

[6] See for example GAO, *Architect of the Capitol: Incorporating All Leading Practices Could Improve Accuracy and Credibility of Projects' Cost Estimates*, GAO–14–333 (Washington, DC: Mar. 25, 2014); *VA Construction: VA Is Working to Improve Initial Project Cost Estimates, but Should Analyze Cost and Schedule Risks*, GAO–10–189 (Washington, DC: Dec. 14, 2009); and *Modernizing the Nuclear Security Enterprise: New Plutonium Research Facility at Los Alamos May Not Meet All Mission Needs*, GAO–12–337 (Washington, DC: Mar. 26, 2012).

[7] See GSA Order 4210.1: CFO P *Cost Estimation Policy Handbook*, June 27, 2007. The GSA Chief Financial Officer initiated this cost estimation policy in response to a GAO recommendation contained in GAO, *Telecommunications: GSA Has Accumulated Adequate Funding for Transition to New Contracts, but Needs Cost Estimation Policy*, GAO–07–268 (Washington, DC: Feb. 23, 2007). Specifically, GSA concurred with a recommendation to establish a policy for cost estimation efforts that reflects leading practices by requiring that estimates be: Comprehensive, well-documented, accurate, and validated.

[8] See for example GAO, *Checked Baggage Screening: TSA Has Deployed Optimal Systems at the Majority of TSA-Regulated Airports, but Could Strengthen Cost Estimates*, GAO–12–266 (Washington, DC: April 27, 2012).

[9] GAO–14–648.

[10] GAO–14–648.

GSA.[11] In addition, OMB's *Capital Programming Guide,* a supplement to OMB Circular A–11, states that Federal agencies must develop sound cost estimates based on the *GAO Cost-Estimating Guide.*[12]

QUESTION FROM CHAIRMAN JEFF DUNCAN FOR CHRIS CUMMISKEY

Question. The GAO report says that "DHS and GSA have not conducted a comprehensive assessment of current needs, identified capability gaps, or evaluated and prioritized alternatives."

With the time frame for completion of 2026 and price tag of $4.5 billion at a minimum, it seems based on GAO's work that St. Elizabeths, as originally envisioned, is unachievable. What is DHS's back-up plan? What are DHS and GSA considering to get this project back on track and save taxpayer dollars?

Answer. With the updated Consolidation Plan currently under review by the administration, DHS and GSA are identifying opportunities to reduce both scope and projected cost in recognition of the changing workplace design standards, the constrained Federal budget environment, and the administration's commitment to reduce the Federal real property portfolio through the "Freeze the Footprint" initiative.

All of the work funded by the Congress and completed to date has been delivered on-time and on-budget. There have been no cost over-runs for funded construction. The General Services Administration (GSA) was required to de-scope certain portions of funded construction contracts to create sufficient capital to complete critical infrastructure that was not funded in 2011 and 2012 to support Phase I occupancy. These actions were fully coordinated and the operational impacts were mitigated through a cooperative effort among GSA and the DHS/United States Coast Guard (USCG) team.

From the Master Plan development up though the completion of Phase I, the Department prohibited requirements changes to allow GSA to effectively manage cost, schedule, and performance.

In their recent testimony before the Committee on Homeland Security, the Government Accountability Office (GAO) acknowledged that while the program did not adhere to their "Leading Practices," published in 1998, the Phase I performance was "effective."

Another step taken to further maximize consolidation is the GSA and DHS collaboration to update the Headquarters Consolidation Plan to address the on-going changes in workplace design and flexible workplace strategies. The DHS Office of the Chief Readiness Support Officer, which manages DHS real property requirements, adopted these strategies and executed a pilot to reduce their office space by 50%, saving over $1 million annually in rent. The lessons learned from this pilot are being implemented as we consolidate space across the country. We anticipate that our final Headquarters Consolidation Plan will significantly reduce space requirements and accommodate more employees than the original plan through the use of flexible workplace strategies. The plan is currently under administration review and will be shared with Congress no later than the submission of the President's fiscal year 2016 budget.

QUESTIONS FROM RANKING MEMBER BENNIE G. THOMPSON FOR CHRIS CUMMISKEY

Question 1. How many locations does the Department occupy in the National Capital Region, and how much of this office space is Federally-owned as opposed to being commercially leased?

Answer. The Department occupies 50 HQ locations in the National Capital Region, including 6 Federally-owned and 44 leased locations as of November 1, 2014.

Question 2. What will GSA and DHS do with the Federally-owned space at the current facility on Nebraska Avenue if the Department vacates it?

Answer. GSA and DHS are planning to continue utilizing this property as part of the Headquarters Consolidation effort. Significant investments have been funded by Congress to improve the infrastructure of the NAC. In addition, several buildings have been renovated, including special space construction for the Office of Intelligence and Analysis (I&A).

Accordingly, our plan seeks to continue to leverage the benefits of occupying Federal space for long-term mission specific needs at lower total ownership costs over leasing.

---

[11] GAO–14–648.

[12] OMB, *Capital Programming Guide, Supplement to OMB Circular A–11,* (Washington, DC: July 2014) and GAO–09–3SP.

QUESTIONS FROM CHAIRMAN JEFF DUNCAN FOR NORMAN DONG

Question 1. The GAO report says that "DHS and GSA have not conducted a comprehensive assessment of current needs, identified capability gaps, or evaluated and prioritized alternatives."

With the time frame for completion of 2026 and price tag of $4.5 billion at a minimum, it seems based on GAO's work that St. Elizabeths, as originally envisioned, is unachievable. What is DHS's back-up plan? What are DHS and GSA considering to get this project back on track and save taxpayer dollars?

Answer. Response was not received at the time of publication.

Question 2. The Food and Drug Administration (FDA) and the General Services Administration (GSA) are working together to consolidate the FDA at the Government-owned White Oak site in Montgomery County, Maryland. Are there lessons learned from GSA's White Oak experience that can be applied to the St. Elizabeths campus?

Answer. Response was not received at the time of publication.

Question 3. To what extent has GSA thoughtfully considered exploring public-private partnerships to help complete/fund the St. Elizabeths campus?

Answer. Response was not received at the time of publication.

Question 4a. GSA has authorities under Section 585 for lease-to-own agreements and under Section 412 for grand lease/lease back agreements. The authorities are hardly ever used especially in recent years.

To what extent has GSA considered using Section 585 and 412 authorities at St. Elizabeths? Are there disincentives for using these authorities?

Answer. Response was not received at the time of publication.

Question 4b. Do you support changing the budget scoring rules to allow for long-term investments in Federal real estate?

Answer. Response was not received at the time of publication.

QUESTION FROM RANKING MEMBER BENNIE G. THOMPSON FOR NORMAN DONG

Question. GSA uses the Automated Prospectus System, or TAPS analysis to make decisions regarding leasing and options for new construction. However, both DHS and GSA have acknowledged that TAPS is not best-suited for the headquarters consolidation.

What other types of analysis have been conducted to make a business case for the new consolidation plan that DHS and GSA are developing, and what did the analysis indicate?

Answer. Response was not received at the time of publication.

○